WHEN IS IT TIME TO QUIT?

Patti Hedgepath Lusk

WHEN IS IT TIME TO QUIT?

Patti Hedgepath Lusk
CounterFlo Ministries
P. O. Box 736
Belton, SC 29627

Printed in the United States of America

Copyright 2020 by Patti Hedgepath Lusk
ISBN 9780578800486
EBOOK 9780578800493

All Scripture quotations are from the New King James Version unless otherwise noted.

All rights reserved. No portion of this book may be used without permission of the author, with the exception of brief excerpts in magazine articles, reviews, etc.

Cover Design by Jason Dorriety
Cover Photo by Jason Dorriety

*This book is dedicated to
my grandsons
who bring more joy to my life
than they could ever imagine.
May you have courage, integrity,
and a relentless trust in Jesus
that will fortify you to never quit,
but remain steadfast in the faith until the end.
I love you.*

TABLE OF CONTENTS

Acknowledgements

Introduction

Chapter 1 Weariness – Elijah, the Prophet

Chapter 2 Red Lights – John, the Beloved

Chapter 3 Adversity – Paul, the Apostle

Chapter 4 Rejection – John Mark

Chapter 5 Acceptance – Jesus

Chapter 6 Envy – The Psalmists

Chapter 7 Circumstances – Bartimaeus, the Blind Man

Chapter 8 Injustice – Joseph

Chapter 9 Hopelessness – Hagar

Chapter 10 Pagan Culture – Daniel

Epilogue

Poem – The Mighty Conqueror

ACKNOWLEDGEMENTS

In June of 1969, Jesus reached down and brought an 11-year-old girl into His kingdom as one of His own. I am overwhelmingly thankful for that night. To know Jesus personally is life itself. I am nothing without Him, and I know that. But I praise God for His Great Treasure in my earthen vessel.

God has also put people in my path who are a source of inspiration, strength and support. Among them is my Mom who reads my writings before anyone else so she can help me remove the 'chaff'. She has spent endless hours over the years without complaint, (except for the wording I use sometimes that makes no sense!) She is also a much needed balance in my life, and a faithful woman of God.

My Daddy was a great man. He was a Marine in World War II who served bravely and faithfully. He was also a great Christian who served the Lord Jesus with courage. He was a man of faith and action. I owe so much to his example.

My husband graciously gives me space when I am in writing mode, and I am grateful for his patience and understanding during these thirty-two years of marriage and ministry. He not only supports my writing endeavors, but we are also partners in ministry in other areas of service. I praise God for bringing us together!

Our son and his wife are special blessings with unique giftings. I am thankful for their love and the many times they have bailed me out of technological problems. Plus they have given us grand children! Our son has been an integral part of our music ministry all his life. What a gift he is.

You would not be holding this book in your hands if it were not for the work of Jason Dorriety who makes sure my books are laid out well, the cover designed, and everything gets in there before it finally goes to print. Many thanks for his willing heart.

I am thankful for you too, my friend, as you embark on this journey with ten of God's people, ordinary people, and see how they faced the difficulties in their lives. With the Lord by their side, they were victorious. I pray the same victory and personal knowledge of our Lord for you.

INTRODUCTION

> **QUIT**
> release hold of something that was in grasp; stop, cease or discontinue; depart from; give up

One day Jesus gave a strong teaching that caused many of the people to stop following Him. When he asked His disciples if they were going to leave Him, too, Peter said, "Lord, to whom shall we go? You have the words of eternal life." Peter remembered his life before Jesus, and he knew how everything had changed since he had begun to follow Him. He probably asked himself, "if we leave Him, what then?" Immediately he had his answer. They had found the Messiah and would not turn away.

Life can be very difficult. Who hasn't felt such despair that they wanted to quit? Yet a glimmer of hope in some souls refuses to die because they have asked themselves "what then?" They know that when they are with Jesus, they are in the best place possible, even with the trials and persecution. When we are tempted to quit, it's time to fan our flame of hope. We can do that by examining the lives of those who had every earthly reason to give up, but every heavenly reason to keep going. Their secret? Their relationship with Jesus Christ, their firsthand knowledge of Him.

Of course, When Is It Time to Quit? is a rhetorical question. We all know it is never time to quit serving Jesus or give up our faith in Him. But we have probably also felt the temptation to give up many times during the heat of the battle. This book will share some of our common battles as Christians and our common solution.

The difference in whether we stand or fall lies in one thing that is so simple few will actually do it. It is to increase our faith and spiritual stamina by maintaining a close relationship with Jesus and His Word. It may sound too simplistic, but that is how each of the examples used in this book prevailed in dire circumstances. Their relationship with God was carefully and consistently maintained, giving them the wisdom, courage and faith to come through the toughest of times. They knew God intimately and trusted Him against all odds. To know Him is to trust Him. To trust Him is to share the fellowship of His suffering and the power of His resurrection. Just as plants with the deepest roots are the hardest to blow over or pull up, so people who have an intimate, active relationship with Jesus are those who "withstand in the evil day".

The Bible explains that the stories told of the people in the Old Testament and the New Testament were written for "our admonition" and as examples for us. He knew that sometimes we need a pattern we can hold up against our circumstances to show us the way. The Bible is full of examples that were recorded specifically for that reason, and in When Is It Time to Quit? We will explore ten of those biblical examples. They dared to put their trust in God…and won!

Chapter One
WEARINESS - ELIJAH, THE PROPHET

> **WEARY**
> tired; without further patience, zeal; to lack courage or lose heart.

A friend of mine had two small children who both got very sick at the same time. Her husband was working an odd shift, and she had no help with the children. While they were both still sick, she caught the virus from them. She laughed later, but said at the time she just began to plan her own funeral.

Have you ever felt that way? Everything seemed to go wrong at once, and you felt as if you were all alone in the world with no hope! We have a choice to make when that happens. We can cave in, turn back, give up and stop where we are, or we can cling to Jesus' hand and brave the storm until we reach the next leg of our journey. The best choice is to go to the next level with the Lord. He will gently renew us and get us through...just like He did for Elijah.

At one point in his ministry, the prophet Elijah faced a situation that stripped him of his zeal and left him "weary in well doing" to the point of asking God to let him die. Maybe he was planning his own funeral, too.

****

We remember the prophet Elijah for his blazing, forceful ministry, raising the widow's dead child back to life, and his ride into heaven in a whirlwind and a chariot of fire. What a mighty servant of God he was! He refused to shrink back from confrontations with Ahab, one of the most wicked kings to ever reign in Israel. Neither did Elijah allow Jezebel, Ahab's wife, to turn him back from being God's fiery spokesman. Jezebel was an instigator of evil that drove her husband even farther into wickedness than his own profane inclinations. She not only had evil intentions, but had the reputation of following through on her threats with no pity for anyone who got in her way.

Because of Ahab's wickedness in building an altar for Baal and worshipping him there, God sent a severe drought on the land. Elijah was God's messenger to Ahab to announce the beginning of the drought. There would be no dew or rain until God proclaimed the drought was over. So, no rain fell for 3 ½ years.

At the end of God's designated time, Elijah was sent back to Ahab with the message that God was going to send rain. Elijah met with Ahab and told him to summon all the people of Israel, the 450 prophets of Baal and the 400 prophets of Asherah to Mount Carmel. When they were gathered together he said, "How long will you falter between two opinions? if the Lord is God, follow Him: but if Baal, follow him."

The challenge was simple and direct. First, the prophets of Baal would build an altar, place the sacrifice on it and then call on Baal to send fire to consume the sacrifice. Then Elijah would do the same and call on the Lord God Jehovah to send fire, "and the God who answers by fire, He is God. So, all the people answered and said, It is well spoken."

The prophets of Baal called on their god from morning until evening. They cut themselves, cried loudly and leaped on the altar. "But there was no voice; no one answered, no one paid attention." It was evident that Baal was not listening. Their god had failed to show any life or power. It had been proven that Baal was not God.

Finally, it was Elijah's turn. He said to all the people, "Come near to me." And the people came near to Elijah. Then he repaired the broken-down altar of the Lord and dug a trench around it. He put the wood and the sacrifice on the altar. Then he ordered them to fill four barrels with water and pour it on the sacrifice and the wood. Three times he had them repeat the process. Wet wood does not catch on fire very well. And there had been an extended drought, so the "waste" of water was probably questionable to the people. But Elijah knew the power of his God, and he knew that rain was on the way. At the time of the offering of the evening sacrifice, Elijah prayed this simple prayer.

"Lord God of Abraham, Isaac, and Israel, let it be known this day that You are God in Israel, I am Your servant, and that I have done all these things at Your word. Hear me, O Lord, hear me, that this people may know that You are the Lord God, and that You have turned their hearts back to You."

Immediately the fire of the Lord fell and consumed the sacrifice, the wet wood, the dust, and even the stones. Then it "licked up the water that was in the trench." Elijah never cut himself. There was no leaping about or crying out in desperation – just obedience and a simple request. And God was listening. That is what happens when we obey God's instructions. We get God's results.

When the people saw what the Lord God had done, they began to cry out, "The Lord, He is God! The Lord, He is God!" Elijah killed all the prophets of Baal that day. Then he prayed for rain, and it poured down breaking the 3 ½ year drought, just as Elijah had prophesied. Two simple prayers. Two miraculous results.

What power was shown through Elijah's obedience! What a great victory was gained in the name of the Lord! Surely this was the time for God to redeem Israel with a revival of repentance. Surely the people would stop dividing their allegiance between God and idols now that they had seen who God is. Even Ahab, Israel's king was there to witness firsthand the power and glory of God.

Ahab had witnessed everything and went home to tell Jezebel about it. When Jezebel heard all that had happened, she sent a messenger to Elijah saying he would be dead by this same time the next day, just like the prophets of Baal.

When Elijah heard this, he ran for his life. He left his servant in Beersheba and went a day's journey into the wilderness. Then he sat down under a juniper tree and made a request to God: "and he requested for himself that he might die; and said, It is enough; now, O Lord, take away my life; for I am not better than my fathers." (KJV) As far as Elijah was concerned, it was time to quit. His days as a prophet were over, finished. But that wasn't his call to make. He did not call himself to be God's prophet, and he could not decide when the call was finished.

Elijah must have felt a flood of emotions – amazement, discouragement, fear, frustration, disappointment…and weariness. It seemed like a good time to quit. He wanted to die, but not at the hand of Jezebel. He had lived long enough, worked long enough, prayed long enough, confronted evil long enough, and preached long enough. He had done enough to bring about a great revival that would turn the nation back to God, but there was no revival and no return to God; just a death threat from Jezebel. The rush of adrenaline and the glow of glory had been darkened with defeat. The victory seemed to have been conquered by evil, allowing wickedness to triumph regardless of God's great display of power and the people's declaration that the Lord was indeed God. Their words meant nothing, and now Elijah was weary. Weary of being the defender.

Weary of being the voice for God that was drowned out by the flood of evil. Weary of preaching a message that never got any results. Elijah was simply weary in well-doing.

It's easy to put ourselves in Elijah's place, because most of us have felt the same way. There may have been times when God opened a door and worked a miracle for us, and we expected great things to come from it. But, let's be honest, sometimes we have been disappointed because the results we expected never came. So, we became weary in doing good and seeing no results.

It happened to the prophet Ezekiel, too. God gave him a word to deliver to His people, but He never promised that there would be significant results. Quite the contrary, God told Ezekiel, "Indeed you are to them as a very lovely song of one who has a pleasant voice and can play well on an instrument; for they hear your words, but they do not do them." (Ezekiel 33:32) However, Ezekiel's words made their way into the Holy Scripture, maybe to prepare us for such times in our own lives.

As Elijah lay sleeping under a juniper tree, an angel touched him and told him to rise and eat. He awoke to find food that had been prepared for him, so he ate and went back to sleep. The angel woke him again and said, "Arise and eat; because the journey is too great for thee."

It is significant that Elijah was under a juniper, because they are evergreens. They stay the same all year round. They are consistently alive and green in cold weather or the scorching sun. Even so, it is not the big miracles that sustain us throughout our lives. It is the consistent sustenance we receive from God on a daily basis. It comes from the steadfastness of our relationship with Him.

God was very gentle and tender with Elijah in his moment of weakness and self-pity. He fed him and let him have time to rest. Then it was time for the moment of self-pity and weariness to come to an end. It was time for Elijah to get up and move on.

So, Elijah got up and ate again, as the angel had told him to do, then he went in the strength of that food for forty days and nights. He went to "Horeb, the mountain of God".

We, as God's servants, are not responsible for the results. We are responsible to be obedient to His word. The final outcome is in God's hands. One person may sow the seed of the Gospel into a heart, another comes to water that word and yet another will reap the harvest. It may seem we have sown in vain if we are the sower of the Word. It may seem we have watered in vain, if we are the one who waters. The one who reaps will have the joy of seeing the harvest here on earth. But they will all have joy and rewards in heaven. We cannot add up the sum of our effectiveness in ministry. God, Who sees clearly the hearts of man, is the only One Who can do that, because He is the only one who knows.

God did not acknowledge Elijah's request to die. That was one prayer uttered by Elijah that God answered with a "No". Neither did the Lord speak to him right away. God knew Elijah's deep disappointment because He knew Elijah's heart. He never chided him for his behavior. He knew Elijah was speaking out of his pain, his weariness and his human frailty, because he felt he had failed in his mission to turn the people back to God; and maybe he was a little disappointed that God had not allowed different results.

Have you ever been so disappointed that you didn't want anyone to try to console you? You didn't want to hear their explanation of how God was going to turn things around? You didn't want to hear them try to come up with a reason thing turned out the way they did? Sometimes words are frustrating and even irritating. We need silence for a while so we can work through the turmoil and adjust our attitude and heart to hear God's voice. God knew Elijah's needs, his loyalty, and his future.

As Elijah lodged in a cave, God finally said, "What are you doing here, Elijah?" Elijah answered, "I have been very zealous for the Lord God of hosts; for the children of Israel have forsaken Your covenant, torn down Your altars, and killed Your prophets with the sword. I alone am left; and they seek to take my life."

Do you feel his heart? It beat for God...the Lord God whom he had given his life to serve. His heart beat for his people who had thrown away their lives by serving idols that had no power, no love, no purpose. The truth was trampled underfoot as the people continued on the path of foolishness and emptiness that led to destruction. Perhaps he had thought things would change. But evil marched on.

You may have felt the same way. Maybe you feel the weariness that goes beyond the physical and seeps all the way through to the spirit. It is a weariness that asks, "what is the use?" It's a weariness that strips your spirit of every ounce of strength and threatens to rob you of your faith. It tears down your courage and causes you to lose heart. All your attempts at sharing the love of Jesus and the power of His Spirit have been met with rejection, and lives remain unchanged. It is a lonely, exhausting feeling.

In response to Elijah's answer, God sent a strong wind, an earthquake and a fire. But God was not in any of these. There is a time for God's might, power and judgment to be shown, but it takes a calm, consistent spirit to follow Him completely in the face of daily living. We have more quiet, average days than days of great victory.

After the demonstration of power shown by these spectacular events was past, God spoke in a "still, small voice". It was a calm, quiet voice such as a "delicate whispering as the breeze among the trees". Have you ever heard that sound? It is incredibly peaceful and soothing. It speaks of something greater than we are and even something mysterious. Yet we know we are safe in His presence. It is the voice of God's Spirit. His voice began to bring focus and purpose back in Elijah's life, and his bitter grief, disappointment and fear began to melt away.

God asked again, "What are you doing here, Elijah?" Elijah's answer was the same as before. When God responded, it was not a rebuke or a reprimand because Elijah had requested to die. Instead, God gave him specific instructions of where to go and what to do.

He was to anoint Hazael to be king over Syria, Jehu to be king over Israel and Elisha to be prophet in Elijah's place. Then God said, "Yet I have left me seven thousand in Israel, all the knees which have not bowed unto Baal, and every mouth which hath not kissed him." (KJV) He let Elijah know that he was not alone. There were others who continued to follow the Lord God. Elijah's ministry was not in vain and it was not over.

There are times in our walk with God when we do not see the results we expected, and so we are ready to give up. We are tired of trying. We are tired of putting forth the effort. We decide it would be easier just to sit back and rest. But God has different plans and He urges us to move forward. He has everything right on schedule, and He needs us to carry out His orders consistently, the times we see results and the times we see none. Only He knows the reasons. Only eternity can prove the true results of our efforts.

We cannot afford to quit when we become weary. Instead of quitting, we have the option of getting in a position to hear from God and receiving nourishment from His Word that will sustain us. "So then faith comes by hearing, and hearing by the word of God." (Romans 10:17) All we need to do is to cling to Him and be quiet for awhile so we can hear His still, small voice speaking in our spirit, melting the grief, disappointment and fear that tries to overwhelm us. Those moments in His presence will renew us and change our perspective.

The disappointment of unfulfilled expectations will shout to us to quit, because evil has overcome. But the soft whisper of God's voice will still every doubt, calm every fear and lead us to our next assignment. He will teach us that true success comes by obeying even when we don't understand.

Strengthened by God and with his focus realigned, Elijah immediately began the task of anointing two kings and training his successor. There was work to be done, and he could not get it done as long as he was hiding in a cave. He could not waste time being discouraged and weary. What was he doing there, anyway? The place where Elijah requested to die became the place where his purpose was renewed. We can label it "burn out" or stress, but he was more like a weary, wounded soldier. He needed to come off the battlefield briefly to be restored to health, then he returned to the battle in full strength with a renewed perspective.

Where are you? And what are you doing there? There is work to be done!

Note: Just to show the justice of God, His accuracy, His timing, and, sometimes, His use of irony: Elijah did not die the next day as Jezebel said. As a matter of fact, he never died. He was taken up to heaven quite alive. However, the testimony of God concerning Jezebel was, "The dogs shall eat Jezebel by the wall of Jezreel." (1 Kings 21:23) We can read how it came to pass in 2 Kings 9:30-37. Justice never comes in our timing, but in God's perfect timing. God's prophecies always come true. Satan's prophecies are idle threats to intimidate God's people, and Satan's prophecies go unfulfilled because he is the father of lies.

****

WHAT ABOUT ME?

Elijah was a man who wholly followed after God. His life was given to pursue God's will above all else. His focus was fixed and his purpose unchanging. In a moment of weakness, he felt defeated, but rose above it because of his relationship with God.

> *"Do not be deceived, God is not mocked; for whatever a man sows, that he will also reap. For he who sows to his flesh will of the flesh reap corruption, but he who sows to the Spirit will of the Spirit*

reap everlasting life. And let us not grow weary while doing good, for in due season we shall reap if we do not lose heart."
Galatians 6:7-9 (KJV)

What factor in my life is most likely to cause me to become "weary in well doing"?

Where is my juniper tree – the place where I seek refuge and plan my own funeral?

In what ways am I sowing to the Spirit?

In what ways am I sowing to the flesh?

> **WORD STUDY**
>
> Flesh – the temporary, weak nature of humanity
>
> Spirit – the eternal, powerful nature of God
>
> Well-doing – to do well, to act for another's benefit.

What part of my lifestyle needs to be rearranged to meet God's priorities?

When I follow after God's principles and directions, what results do I expect from Him and other people?

Chapter Two

RED LIGHTS – JOHN, THE BELOVED

> **RED LIGHT**
> traffic light that signals a traveler to stop; to cease motion or activity; to block or prevent

My Daddy was in the Marines for four years during World War II. For nearly a year, he and about 300 other Marines were stationed on a small island in the Pacific. They were not told why they were sent there and never knew the full purpose of their mission. But they risked their lives to defend that island against enemy attacks and held it under American control because they were commissioned to do so. For several months of that year, they received no supplies or food from the outside and had to rely on fish from the ocean and fruit on the island for nourishment. No matter how difficult their circumstances, they remained faithful to the assignment. They knew their orders came from the commanding officers who saw the whole scope of the war, not just one battle.

God often sends us on missions that we don't understand, and He doesn't always explain the details. But we can rest assured that He sees the whole scope of things and knows the significance of the mission He entrusts to us. During those times, it is important to listen closely, trust and obey. We might not understand His assignment, but we can be sure of His wisdom and His love for us. Everything He leads us to do will benefit His Kingdom.

He sent John, the Beloved Disciple, to an island on assignment, too.

****

Some seasons of our lives are like red lights. They always catch us when we are in a hurry, and they waste precious time we could use for something else. The more we have on our schedule to do, the longer the red light seems to last. They can bring out impatience in the best of us. Some of us even try to find a different route so we can avoid them.

Red lights! Who needs them? To be honest, we all need them. Think about how it would be if there were no red lights. We would face danger and chaos at every crossroad.

God strategically places "red lights" in our lives for our good and for His glory. Just when it seems we are flowing well in the traffic of life, we come to a red light. We have a choice. We can run it and risk a collision, whine until it turns green, or use the time to draw closer to God and wait in His presence until we get the 'go' signal from Him.

The times we see as our "down times" can be some of our most profitable if we recognize them for what they are. In other words, when no doors are open for us to walk through, that is the time to be still and open the door of our spirit to God. That gives Him access to work in us however He wants to work. I read a church sign that said, "If you cannot pray a door open, don't try to pry it open." That is a succinct bit of wisdom we would all do well to follow.

John, the Beloved, one of Jesus' twelve disciples, experienced this principle in a spectacular way late in his life. He learned how life-changing a red light can be.

John had a wonderful resume. He was the son of Zebedee and brother of James. He and James were fishermen and partners with Simon Peter and his brother Andrew. It seems they had a profitable business, but all four of these men left their livelihood to follow Jesus Christ. "So when they had brought their boats to land, they forsook all and followed Him." (Luke 5:11, italics added)

Peter, James and John were the inner circle of Jesus' twelve disciples. We all have a circle of friends we are closer to than others, and these three were Jesus' closest friends.

They were the only ones allowed to go in with Jesus when He raised Jairus' daughter from the dead. They were the only ones with Him on the Mount of Transfiguration. And it was Peter, James and John who were nearest to Him in the Garden of Gethsemane. There are several references to John being "the disciple whom Jesus loved"; and from the cross, Jesus committed His mother into John's keeping. That reflected the confidence Jesus had in John.

John was a witness to Jesus' death on the cross and of His resurrection. He saw Him many times after He arose. He also witnessed Christ's ascension and was among those in the Upper Room when the Holy Ghost was poured out as Jesus had promised. John and Peter healed a man in Jesus' name and were put in jail because of it. When the persecution became severe in Jerusalem and many of the Christians scattered, John stayed in Jerusalem. Later, he became a missionary to Samaria.

As we continue reading his resume, we find that John wrote one of the four gospels, three epistles and the book of Revelation. He worked miracles, signs and wonders, preached the Word and gave testimony of Christ to many people; and this is just a small portion of his resume. He was busy doing the work of God's Kingdom. Then came the red light!

It was during the time of the Roman persecution of Christians (about A.D. 95) that John was arrested and exiled for proclaiming Christianity. His role in the proclamation of the Kingdom of God was important, and he was faithfully carrying it out just as Jesus had told them. Yet, suddenly, he was taken away from his work and from people who needed to hear his message, and was exiled on an island. Certainly, this was the work of Satan to cause such persecution of Christians, but God did not stop it. He allowed it. In the earlier years of the persecution, Peter had been arrested and then released from prison by a miracle. Paul and Silas experienced the same miraculous power that set them free. But for John, there was no such miracle. God did not release him from the hands of the authorities who took him to exile. God did, however, have a greater miracle in the making.

John wrote about his exile experience like this: "I, John, both am your brother and companion in the tribulation, and kingdom and patience of Jesus Christ, was on the island that is called Patmos for the word of God and for the testimony of Jesus Christ." (Revelation 1:9)

Patmos was a small, rocky island off the southwest coast of Asia Minor. It was fifteen miles in circumference and barren. That is where this active, powerful man of God found himself. He was in a barren wasteland surrounded by water. There was no escape.

If we look at his circumstance in the natural, we see the end of John's ministry. How could it be God's will that he be taken away from the multitudes that needed to hear his message of the Kingdom of God? How could God allow him to experience such harsh treatment? John was also removed from the companionship of the other believers. There were none to encourage him or pray with him. How devastating!

What about Romans 8:28? Didn't God give us that promise? "And we know that all things work together for good to those who love God, to those who are the called according to His purpose." John surely fell into that category, but there seemed to be no way anything good could come from this experience.

God saw his circumstance in a different light – the right light! This was not an end to ministry. It was another component in the whole spectrum of John's calling. John had been taken away from the multitudes of his day and time because he was being called to minister to those in a different day and time (you and me included), not just another culture. John found himself on this island in direct fellowship with Jesus Christ. He was still in the inner circle.

What did John do with his experience? He did the same thing he did when he was in the middle of all the activity. His communication with Jesus was his vital Source then, and that did not change.

This is what he wrote. "I was in the Spirit on the Lord's Day, and I heard behind me a loud voice, as of a trumpet". 'The Lord's Day' is simply a period of time belonging to the Lord. It is usually associated with a Sabbath. This was the red light, the time to cease activity and spend time in God's presence. Jesus needed John to Himself for awhile and He knew John well enough to know what he would do in this situation. John drew close to Jesus, and even his time on Patmos was transformed into a miracle through which many generations would hear the Truth and see the future open up in an astounding way. John received a different kind of miracle than the ones Peter, Paul and Silas had received.

God was about to remove the blinders and reveal Jesus Christ in all His glory. John had known Him closely in human flesh, but he had never seen Him like this before. His description of Jesus is magnificent. He saw Him as the conquering King rather than the Suffering Servant.

"Then I turned to see the voice that spoke with me. And having turned I saw seven golden lampstands, and in the midst of the seven lampstands One like the Son of Man, clothed with a garment down to the feet and girded about the chest with a golden band. His head and hair were white like wool, as white as snow, and His eyes like a flame of fire; His feet were like fine brass, as if refined in a furnace, and His voice as the sound of many waters; He had in His right hand seven stars, out of His mouth went a sharp two-edged sword, and His countenance was like the sun shining in its strength." (Revelation 1:12-16) What a glorious vision of Jesus Christ! He was overwhelming in His splendor and brilliance. John said, "And when I saw Him, I fell at His feet as dead. But He laid His right hand on me, saying to me, "Do not be afraid; I am the First and the Last. I am He who lives, and was dead, and behold, I am alive forevermore. Amen. And I have the keys of Hades and of Death." (Revelation 1:17-18)

For those of us who desire a revelation of Jesus Christ, it will come when we draw ourselves into the presence of God. It happens when we enter the period of time that belongs to the Lord, and we cease our activity so we can see Him and hear Him alone. That is when He will accomplish what He wants to accomplish in us. Our vision of Christ won't be exactly like John's, but it will be the revelation we need in order to truly know Him as He is and to make Him known to others as we know Him.

What if John had decided to quit seeking God because God had taken him away from his ministry? What if he had not been in the spirit on the Lord's day? What do we miss when we pull away from God's presence?

John didn't have time to give up. He had work to do. Jesus showed John a breathtaking vision and told him to "Write the things which you have seen, and the things which will take place after this". (Revelation 1:19)

How could John know what an impact his exile experience would have on future generations – millions of people down through the ages of time? Possibly, he never knew in his lifetime how wide-reaching his "red light" experience would extend. Because he remained in close contact with Jesus through his times of trial and obscurity, he received a magnificent personal experience and a tremendous mandate. That is how God fulfills His Romans 8:28 promise. When we truly "love God" and are "the called according to His purpose", we will see good come from the worst of circumstances.

Learning to listen to Jesus is a choice that is born out of desire. Sometimes we get too busy and don't take time to be with Him. We are in a hurry to get this done or that done and have our schedule carefully prepared. If we are too rigid with our own agenda, we may miss working with God, for the sake of working "for" God. It's a poor trade-off.

I used to go to my grandmother's house for lunch. On one of those occasions, I ate lunch and hurriedly left to return to work. Later I learned that as I was leaving, my grandmother had been tapping on the window to wave a final farewell to me. My attention had already shifted to other things, and I didn't notice she was trying to get my attention.

How often we quickly read our Bible and pray, then hurriedly go our way. As soon as we leave that quiet place, our thoughts turn toward other things; and we do not notice Jesus tapping on our hearts. We do not ignore Him out of malice but out of carelessness.

Another obstacle to listening to Jesus is to be so caught up with the end goal that we miss all the opportunities between here and there.

The pace of this world is so fast that we can barely keep up. It can be like a roller coaster ride with its ups and downs, turns and twists, and hills that take our breath. But remember, our faith is weak when our relationship with Christ is weak. Our strength is weak when our relationship with Christ is weak. We are more susceptible to quitting when we stop abiding in Christ and just visit Him from time to time. The empty, lonely feeling within is a longing for His presence. If we deprive ourselves from entering into His presence, we become fearful, weary, distracted and restless. Many people try to quicken the pace of life to fill that longing, but only Jesus can fill that void.

When we choose, like John, to consistently live in His presence, our faith and strength will be increased daily and we will eventually see good come from everything we experience. Every experience may not be good in itself, but God will bring something good out of it eventually. We will see the purposes of God worked through us and our circumstances when we least expect it.

Have you come up on a red light today? Barrenness all around you? Loneliness? Lost opportunities? This is no time to quit. It is no time to give up. It is time to seek the Lord. It is not the end. It could be the beginning of a new phase of life God has for you. One door may be closed to turn your attention to the one God has opened for you. Don't take the exit. Just wait in God's presence until He opens the next door.

Red lights can be used as a transition to end one phase of our calling and begin another one. After over 26 years in the radio ministry, I felt discouraged and empty when it was over. I was not sure who I was or what my purpose was. But I remember praying, "Here I am, Lord, send me." Later, as I sat in a seminar, God spoke to me to write a specific book. I wrote that book, three more books, recorded a CD with my family and expanded the television ministry we were involved with. My transition from radio was painful and confusing. I felt that my ministry was over, but God gave me my next assignments. He is faithful.

Oswald Chambers said, "There are times when you cannot understand why you cannot do what you want to do. When God brings the blank space, see that you do not fill it in, but wait."

There are times when Jesus calls us to rest in Him. But when it's time to work, we need to be sure we are working alongside Him and not trying to carry it out on our own. Working with Jesus lessens the struggle of the labor. "Come to Me, all you who labor and are heavy laden, and I will give you rest. Take my yoke upon you, and learn from Me, for I am gentle and lowly in heart; and you will find rest for your souls." (Matthew 11:28-29) The Sabbath rest is fulfilled in trusting our lives into God's hands and ceasing from our own works. (See Hebrews 4:9-10) When we become anxious, worried and upset, we break the rest Jesus has for us. But He invites us to "come". We can be "in the Spirit" during the time that belongs to the Lord just as John was.

Jesus called John aside for a timeless task, but it looked like a disaster at first. "Mark one up for the enemy". No, it was not the enemy that won. God won. John won. You, me and every other person who has ever read or ever will read the book of the Revelation of Jesus Christ won because of John's red light. And because God took what the enemy meant for evil and turned it for good.

John wrote what he saw and heard. He wrote about Jesus, the Lamb of God, as he had known Him on earth in the gospel that bears his name. Then he wrote about Jesus, the King of kings and Lord of lords, as he saw Him on the Isle of Patmos – the Revelation of Jesus Christ!

Your Patmos is just a red light, a temporary pause. Take full advantage of it, for it is a facet of your life designed by God, just as surely as John's red light was designed for him. Recognize it as a period of time belonging to the Lord. It will give you a fresh revelation at the crossroad before you continue on your journey.

Note: Historians tell us John was released from Patmos the year after he was sent there (A.D. 96) and returned to Ephesus where he remained until his death. He was the only one of the twelve apostles to die a natural death as an old man.

****

WHAT ABOUT ME?

We all have an idea of what we consider usefulness in the Kingdom of God. When something comes to take us away from that perception, we struggle mentally and emotionally. Yet, God needs us to be quiet and come away from the busyness of life periodically so we can hear him.

"And He [Jesus] said unto them [the disciples], Come ye yourselves into a desert place, and rest a while: for there were many coming and going and they had no leisure so much as to eat." Mark 6:31

What "red light" has God allowed in my life?

What is my biggest struggle with "down time" (my emotional reaction)?

How can I overcome the struggle and replace it with God's perspective of my situation?

Am I taking time to hear God's voice and His direction?

> **WORD STUDY**
>
> Apart – away from the crowds and to one's self; privacy
>
> Desert – place of solitude
>
> Rest – ease, refreshment
>
> While – brief period of time

Jesus called the disciples to come apart with Him to rest. Do I follow the message of this scripture passage, or am I disregarding it? In what ways?

When is the last time I have had a fresh revelation of Jesus? How did it affect my daily life?

Chapter Three

ADVERSITY – PAUL

> **ADVERSITY**
> hostility,
> opposition,
> attacks from
> an enemy,
> ill treatment,
> persecution,
> to pursue

I used to have a cat named Robo. My daddy named him on the way to the vet one day when we realized he would need a name for the vet's medical records when we got there. Robo was a tough cat - a stocky, gray tabby - who seemed to always be in a fight. I was constantly nursing him back to health from his escapades, because he was fully committed to defend his territory. He forcefully held his ground and bore the scars bravely. His ears were tattered and he had a bad wound on his head that never seemed to get completely well before his next battle. Still, Robo remained faithful regardless of the cost.

How faithful are we to the gospel of Jesus Christ? Are we willing to bear the scars of a warrior, to pay the price of being citizens of the Kingdom of God, yet still living in this world? Our warfare is not in the flesh, but in the spirit. Jesus has won the battle and gained ground for us. Our responsibility is to stand and hold our territory. It takes perseverance to stand our ground against the forces of evil. But one day all our wounds will be healed and we will receive a reward that will never fade away.

Robo was faithful to keep all the territory that was his, even at great cost to himself. He was persistent and endured all the attacks and hostility so he could hold his ground. He had a specific goal and he stuck with it.

The Apostle Paul was persistent, too, but his goal was a much higher calling. The territory he held was a mandate from God to take the gospel message to the Gentiles, kings and the Jews. Paul was faithful to keep all the territory that was his, even at great cost to himself.

****

Saul of Tarsus was brought up in strict adherence to the law and traditions of his Jewish heritage. In Philippians 3:5-6, he explains it like this: "Circumcised the eighth day, of the stock of Israel, of the tribe of Benjamin, a Hebrew of the Hebrews; concerning the law, a Pharisee; concerning zeal, persecuting the church; concerning the righteousness which is in the law, blameless." Saul was taught the law at the feet of Gamaliel, a Pharisee and doctor of the law who was highly respected by all the people. As you can see, Saul's credentials were flawless.

In this environment of tradition and religious pageantry, a "new Way" was being preached. Many of the Jewish people were turning from the established synagogues and teachers to follow the teachings of Jesus of Nazareth Who had died by crucifixion. However, His followers claimed He was alive, that He had risen from the dead. There were a lot of strange happenings such as healings and miracles that had the crowds mesmerized, the same types of iracles Jesus had performed before His death. The disciples of Jesus were proclaiming His teachings to the people, and the people were accepting them above the traditions taught by the scribes and Pharisees. As they saw it, their way of life was in danger.

With Saul's staunch background and training, he felt he had an obligation to protect and defend the Jewish law and traditions, so he began to persecute the followers of Jesus Christ. He was standing by when the first of Jesus' followers was put to death. He heard Stephen's message and watched as the enraged religious rulers begin to "gnash on him with their teeth" because of their anger against the truth. But when Stephen cried out, "Look! I see the heavens opened and the Son of Man standing at the right hand of God!" they took him out to stone him. Saul heard him say, "Lord Jesus, receive my spirit" as they were stoning him. He watched as he knelt down, and he heard him cry out, "Lord, do not charge them with this sin." Then he saw him die. "Now Saul was consenting to his death."

Despite the persecution, this new Way was spreading quickly. Saul was an educated, respected Pharisee who was zealous to defend the law. He believed the traditions of his people with his whole heart and had given his entire life studying them, teaching them and keeping them. He saw this Way as a threat to all he believed, and he had to do something about it. After all, the whole religious structure was being undermined.

"Then Saul, still breathing threats and murder against the disciples of the Lord, went to the high priest." He asked for letters of permission to go to the synagogues in Damascus and bring back any of "this way" who were infiltrating the Jewish belief with their doctrine. He would arrest both men and women. He was granted his request.

Earlier, when some of the apostles had been arrested for preaching Jesus and healing people in Jerusalem, they had been brought before the high priest and the Jewish council. These men wanted to kill them. But Gamaliel, Saul's former mentor, gave them this advice: "And he said to them: "Men of Israel, take heed to yourselves what you intend to do regarding these men. For some time ago Theudas rose up, claiming to be somebody. A number of men, about four hundred, joined him. He was slain, and all who obeyed him were scattered and came to nothing. After this man, Judas of Galilee rose up in the days of the census, and drew away many people after him. He also perished, and all who obeyed him were dispersed. And now I say to you, keep away from these men and let them alone; for if this plan or this work is of men, it will come to nothing; but if it is of God, you cannot overthrow it—lest you even be found to fight against God." (Acts 5:35-39)

I find that passage interesting, and I wonder what Gamaliel thought about his zealous student Saul. The council accepted Gamaliel's advice on that occasion, but later Saul was able to get letters from the High Priest that gave him authority to arrest Christians and bring them back to Jerusalem in bonds. Saul would soon discover Gamaliel was right. He found himself fighting against The Lord Jesus Christ.

As Saul was on his journey to Damascus with these letters that we may call warrants, he had an extraordinary experience. A light from heaven shone all around him. He fell to the ground and heard a voice say, "Saul, Saul, why are you persecuting Me?" Saul asked, "Who are You, Lord?" Notice he called Him Lord. He didn't know who it was, but he recognized His authority. "Then the Lord said, I am Jesus Whom you are persecuting. It is hard for you to kick against the goads." A goad is a spur or an instrument used to drive an animal in the desired direction. Jesus told Saul it would turn out badly if he kept resisting God's direction.

Have you ever been there? Or should I rather ask how many times have we all been there? We set our sights on a certain goal and run for it. We think, "Surely this is what God wants me to do, but we don't take time to ask. Then He gets our attention. We fall to the ground, see the light and finally hear His voice. It is hard to go against what God is for, or to try to accomplish what God is against.

Notice Jesus did not say Saul was persecuting His people. He said he was persecuting Him. When someone mistreats one of God's children, Jesus takes it personally. Although Saul had been thoroughly convinced that he was doing God a service, in reality he had ceased to follow God's law when he determined to fight against God's plan. He did it unknowingly and out of sincerity for what he believed. He was well-intentioned, zealous for his God, sincere, and wrong!

The very thing he thought was trying to annihilate his God's law was actually the fulfillment of it. His knowledge and impressive credentials were not enough to reveal the truth to him. But Jesus revealed Himself to Saul that day on the road to Damascus. Jesus – the merciful Savior! The God of grace!We all have been mistaken in our beliefs at one time or another, some on a larger scale than others. But God is faithful to correct those who have sincere, open hearts. He has a way of redirecting our zeal into the right channel if we let Him. When God does something to get our attention, it may not have the intensity of Saul's Damascus Road experience, but it will be every bit as life-changing.

Trembling and astonished, Saul answered, "Lord, what do You want me to do?" God had his attention. Saul was through following his own agenda and asked for God's will. Now he was willing to do whatever Jesus said. He was given instructions to go into the city where he would be told what to do next. When Saul got up from the ground, he was blind and had to be led into the city by the men who were with him.

When Jesus reveals Himself to us, there is no doubt as to His Lordship. He gains our full attention, and suddenly our sole desire is to make ourselves completely available to Him. The things we thought were so important fade into obscurity when we find the truth.

God had also spoken to one of His faithful disciples in Damascus and told him to go and pray for Saul. He was probably one of the ones Saul was coming to arrest. At first, Ananias was reluctant to go on that mission because he had heard all about Saul and the damage he intended to do to the church. "But the Lord said to him, Go for he is a chosen vessel of Mine, to bear my name before Gentiles, kings, and the children of Israel: For I will show him how many things he must suffer for My name's sake."

Ananias went and prayed for Saul, and Saul became a mighty voice in the Kingdom of God. The combination of being an expert on

Old Testament scriptures and meeting Jesus face to face made Saul the perfect witness of the fact that Jesus really is the Messiah!

Almost immediately after his encounter with Jesus, he began to preach in the synagogues that Jesus is the Christ. And, almost immediately, the persecutor became the persecuted just as the Lord had said. But the persecution did not deter him from his calling. Saul followed Jesus even more diligently than he had the traditions of his heritage. He was no longer called Saul, but was referred to throughout the rest of the scriptures as Paul. An interesting footnote in my Bible mentions that the name Saul meant 'destroyer' and the name Paul meant 'worker'. Matthew Henry notes that Saul was his Hebrew name, and as a Pharisee among his people he was called by that name. However, when he was called to go to the Gentiles, he used his Roman name, Paul. For whatever reason his name was changed, Paul was a very different man and did the works of God often through great adversity.

Later in his ministry, Paul wrote of his many persecutions. "From the Jews five times I received forty stripes minus one. Three times I was beaten with rods; once I was stoned; three times I was shipwrecked; a night and a day I have been in the deep; in journeys often, in perils of waters, in perils of robbers, in perils of my own countrymen, in perils of the Gentiles, in perils in the city, in perils in the wilderness, in perils in the sea, in perils among false brethren; in weariness and toil, in sleeplessness often, in hunger and thirst, in fastings often, in cold and nakedness— besides the other things, what comes upon me daily: my deep concern for all the churches." (2 Corinthians 11:24-28) Paul's load was staggering, but he referred to it as a "light affliction, which is but for a moment." (2 Corinthians 4:17)

Instead of reading quickly through the list, look carefully at each circumstance he endured. If we endured just one of those adversities, how would we respond? Would we quit following Jesus, or could we still rejoice?

Paul was tenacious in preaching what he believed, because it was more than the letter of the law. He had met Jesus face to face, and through the fellowship of the Spirit, he had learned much "at Jesus feet".

What have we learned at the feet of Jesus? How attentive are we to His voice? The decision to be one with Jesus will make all the difference in how we live our lives, spend our time, use our resources and in the person we will become. It will forever change our concept of what is truly important. When we are fully persuaded that something is right and of great value, we must stand our ground regardless of the consequences.

Paul had complete confidence that the Lord would bring him through every adversity. This confidence was born of and sustained by his past experience and his ongoing revelation of Jesus. Second Corinthians 4:8-9 offers us a little more insight into the foundation of his unyielding trust.

"We are troubled on every side, yet not distressed; we are perplexed, but not in despair; Persecuted, but not forsaken; cast down, but not destroyed." (KJV)

If we are troubled, we are hedged in. Have you ever felt that way? Trapped by a circumstance? Or maybe the opposition of the people around you made you feel anxious and boxed in. Sometimes we feel that the walls are closing in around us and will soon crush us, but God will deliver us. Remember, we may be "troubled on every side", but God will not allow us to be crushed.

I saw an old movie once where the "bad guys" captured the "good guys" and put them in a room where the walls began to close in on them. The room was built to crush grapes, but the purpose of the enemy was to torture their minds and finally crush them to death. It certainly made for some heart-pounding drama, but the "good guys" escaped in the end. In Psalm 118, the psalmist says when he was in trouble (a tight spot), he cried out to God and "the Lord answered me, and set me in a large place." (KJV) How refreshing when we are taken out of that tight spot and put in an open place of freedom. Keep your faith in Jesus Christ. He will not allow anything to crush you. It may be tight sometimes, but God is faithful.

Then Paul says "we are perplexed, but not in despair". The word "perplexed" here means to be without a way. But the words "not in despair" mean not utterly without a way. When our circumstances look impossible, we tend to doubt and get upset. We become anxious. That is when our human nature takes over and tries to design a way out only to realize there is no way out. But God is not without a way, so we are not utterly without a way. We have the resources of God when we belong to Jesus. We may not have a way out in our own strength and wisdom, but we are not without resources when we are following Jesus. As my friend often says, "God has ways we don't know anything about."

Next, Paul mentions persecution. As we have learned, he was very familiar with persecution, but he was equally familiar with the

Comforter, the Holy Spirit, Who stands by us. We may be pursued by the enemy, but we will never be forsaken by our Lord. I don't like lightening. When we have a storm with thunder and lightning at night, I move a little closer to my husband. I find comfort in his presence. We can move closer to Jesus and find comfort in His presence during times of persecution. He will never desert us or leave us behind to stand alone. Psalm 23 tells us He will prepare a table for us in the very presence of our enemies. Remember when Stephen was stoned to death? As he was dying he saw "the glory of God, and Jesus standing on the right hand of God." (Acts 7:55 KJV) He was not deserted and neither will be any of God's servants.

Paul also says we may be cast down (struck to the ground), but we will not be destroyed (destroyed fully, perish). When we are cast down, it is not a permanent position. "The steps of a good man are ordered by the LORD, And He delights in his way. Though he fall, he shall not be utterly cast down; For the LORD upholds him with His hand." (Psalm 37:23-24) God will raise us up in spite of the enemy's attempts to keep us down.

When you feel overwhelmed, re-read this passage of Scripture. It was inspired by the Holy Ghost and written by the pen of one who had experienced it all and found God faithful.

If anyone had a reason to quit, Paul did; but he found hope and strength in Christ and was determined to complete everything God had for him to do. He would not let any territory that God had placed under his stewardship go without the gospel message, regardless of the cost to himself. He did not want to be lacking in anything when he stood before the Lord.

After listing some of his adversities and proclaiming that the Lord had delivered him out of them all, Paul wrote: "Yes, and all who desire to live godly in Christ Jesus will suffer persecution." (2 Timothy 3:12)

Why do the godly suffer persecution? We suffer persecution in this life because there is a spiritual war going on and this world is the battlefield. We are not of this world, yet we are in it. Jesus explained it this way, "If you were of the world, the world would love its own. Yet because you are not of the world, but I chose you out of the world, therefore the world hates you." (John 15:19) Satan fights against every true servant of God. That is why Paul's ministry was riddled with bullet holes shot from the enemy's weapon. Paul was a vital link in the chain of spreading the gospel to future generations – all the way to our generation.

When Jesus called Paul to be a chosen vessel for Him, He told him he would suffer great things for His name's sake. Jesus makes it clear that persecution is a fact for the true child of God; not to frighten us or cause us to live with a martyr syndrome hanging over us like a dark cloud. He told us so we won't be caught off guard or misunderstand what is happening to us. An old adage says "forewarned is forearmed".

Paul was not caught off guard by the persecution. He was prepared, so he continued on the path Jesus set for him regardless of the obstacles. That is why when he determined the Lord would have him go to Jerusalem, he would not let anyone dissuade him. He was compelled in his spirit to go to Jerusalem and eventually to Rome. Paul didn't choose to suffer. He chose to do the will of God even if it meant he would suffer.

On his journey to Jerusalem, Paul went to Miletus. While he was there, he sent a message to Ephesus and asked the elders of the church to come to him. During his farewell address to them, he said, "And see, now I go bound in the spirit to Jerusalem, not knowing the things that will happen to me there, except that the Holy Spirit testifies in every city, saying that chains and tribulations await me. But none of these things move me; nor do I count my life dear to myself, so that I may finish my race with joy, and the ministry which I received from the Lord Jesus, to testify to the gospel of the grace of God." The threats of imprisonment did not change what was etched in his spirit.

Have you ever felt God nudge you to do something and fear arose or someone's doubt caused you to second-guess His plans? Maybe you felt a drawing to speak to a certain person or venture out further than you were comfortable doing. In those times, listen to what God's Spirit is whispering in your spirit. God doesn't use fear tactics. He is a God of order and will give a solid 'yes' deep within even when your mind has reservations. Learn to follow the voice of God within you.

One night, during my time with the Lord, I felt compelled to take a step that was very different for me. While in the presence of the Lord, it was exciting. But the next morning, when it was time to do what the Lord had prompted me to do, I was afraid and began to feel that it couldn't possibly work. Suddenly what had seemed not only possible, but even a reality, seemed completely impossible. I felt foolish for thinking even for a moment that it would work out. Then I remembered the passage of scripture He had given me the night before. It was a warning that fear would try to overtake me when it was time to act on God's guidance. So, I followed through regardless of the doubt, because I believed God had spoken to me and had given me His word of encouragement.

Paul was following the voice of the Spirit within him. He was also following the example of Jesus. Jesus had known when it was time to start back toward Jerusalem, and He knew what would eventually happen there. Since the Jews were plotting to kill Him, He had stayed away from Jerusalem because it was not yet His time to die. His disciples tried to keep Him from going back because they feared the Jews' would kill Him. His brothers (who did not believe in Him at that time) sarcastically challenged Him to go and reveal Himself. Jesus was unmoved by the disciples' fear and his brothers' unbelief. He kept His eyes on the Father and set his face to go to Jerusalem when the time was right. "Now it came to pass, when the time had come for Him to be received up, that He steadfastly set His face to go to Jerusalem." (Luke 9:51) He knew what awaited Him there, but His life was committed to the will of the Father, not the will of His humanity.

When Jesus told His disciples what would happen to Him in Jerusalem, "Then Peter took Him aside and began to rebuke Him, saying, "Far be it from You, Lord; this shall not happen to You!" But He turned and said to Peter, "Get behind Me, Satan! You are an offense to Me, for you are not mindful of the things of God, but the things of men." (Matthew16:22-23)

Much like Jesus, as Paul drew closer to Jerusalem, Agabus, a prophet from Judea, came to him. He took Paul's belt and bound himself with it and said, "Thus says the Holy Spirit, 'So shall the Jews at Jerusalem bind the man who owns this belt, and deliver him into the hands of the Gentiles." All the people cried and begged Paul not to go, but Paul had to obey God. We probably would have considered the words of Agabus to be a warning not to go to Jerusalem. But, Paul had a clear view of God's direction, and would not let the requests of others or the ominous words of the prophet prevent him from continuing. Now he knew what would happen when he got there, but he also knew the Spirit was telling him to go. He had been forewarned through the prophets' words and would be prepared. He probably remembered the warning from God given to him through Ananias so many years before: "For I will show him how many things he must suffer for My name's sake."

When Paul arrived in Jerusalem, he was indeed arrested just as Agabus prophesied. Some of the Jews who knew him and the message he preached, saw him and incited a riot. They were beating Paul and the Romans came to rescue him by arresting him. That night the Lord stood beside Paul and said, "Be of good cheer, Paul; for as you have testified for Me in Jerusalem, so you must also bear witness at Rome." What encouragement! He knew he would not die in Jerusalem, because he had an appointment in Rome just as he had believed.

Paul was eventually escorted out of Jerusalem with an entourage of 200 soldiers, 70 horsemen and 200 spearmen. There was a death threat against him that became known to the chief captain, and he sent Paul by night to Felix, the governor in Caesarea.

Felix said he would hear Paul's case when his accusers arrived. They came and stated their accusation and Paul was allowed to give his defense. Felix made no decision at that time, but "he commanded a centurion to keep Paul, and to let him have liberty, and that he should forbid none of his acquaintance to minister or come unto him." (KJV)

Felix brought Paul to talk with him on many occasions, but never released him. After two years, Felix was replaced by Festus and Paul remained imprisoned. The Jews asked Festus to send Paul to Jerusalem to stand trial, but they were planning to kill him on the way. When Festus asked Paul if he would go, he said he would not and he appealed to Caesar.

Before Paul was sent to Caesar, King Agrippa came to visit with Felix, and Paul was brought before them. When King Agrippa heard Paul speak, he said, "This man might have been set free if he had not appealed to Caesar." It may seem Paul had made a terrible mistake. He could have been a free man except for those four little words he had spoken – "I appeal unto Caesar." We probably would have felt like a terrible failure if we found ourselves in that situation, but Paul knew he was going to Rome, one way or another. I believe he knew it was part of God's plan.

How many times have we said "if only I hadn't…"? Just maybe God used what we thought was a mistake to get us to the right place. We may have been convinced that we prevented God's plan, but God may have allowed it to bring us to the place He designed us to be. In Paul's case, his "if only I hadn't appealed to Caesar" was the catalyst to fulfill God's plan for him to go to Rome.

Paul finally arrived at Rome, but not before he endured a shipwreck, the threat of all the prisoners being killed, finding refuge on an island, and receiving a snake bite that would have killed Paul except for the protection of the Lord. All these adversities opened doors for Paul to minister to others and share the gospel message. And that was just on the journey to his destination. I wonder how many opportunities we miss along our journey because we are waiting until we reach another place? After arriving in Rome, Paul was assigned a guard and allowed to live by himself rather than with the other prisoners.

After three days, he called together the chief of the Jews to come hear his case (and his testimony). They were not angered by his message, but neither did they receive it. "Then Paul dwelt two whole years in his own rented house, and received all who came to him, 31 preaching the kingdom of God and teaching the things which concern the Lord Jesus Christ with all confidence, no one forbidding him." (Acts 28:30-31) Paul wrote many of his letters while he was imprisoned. History tells us that Paul was eventually beheaded.

The Christian walk is not always an easy one, but it is always a blessed one. God blesses those who set themselves apart for Him and endure to the end. With our faith fixed on Jesus Christ we can come to the end of our lives and say, like Paul, "For I am now ready to be offered, and the time of my departure is at hand. I have fought a good fight, I have finished my course, I have kept the faith: Henceforth there is laid up for me a crown of righteousness, which the Lord, the righteous judge, shall give me at that day: and not to me only, but unto all them also that love his appearing." (2 Timothy 4:6-8)

****

WHAT ABOUT ME?

Although Paul's life was riddled with trials and tribulation, he found great fulfillment and joy in serving Jesus Christ. We can find that same joy as we go about our "Father's business". We may not always be popular, but we can find peace in Christ as we stand firmly in Him. After experiencing a life of persecution and opposition, Paul was able to say without reservation:

> *"Be anxious for nothing, but in everything by prayer and supplication, with thanksgiving, let your requests be made known to God."* Philippians 4:6

Have I learned how to stand when it seems everything and everyone is against me?

Am I faithful to truth even when it makes others angry?

How do I handle anxiety? Do I let it discourage me from continuing in the Lord's work, or do I take it to the Lord and let His peace (oneness with Him) guard my mind and give me assurance?

Do I recognize the voice of God speaking in my spirit?

> **Word Study**
>
> Anxious – worried, uneasy
>
> Peace – being at one with God
>
> Keep – guard

Chapter Four

REJECTION – JOHN MARK

> **REJECTION**
> disapproval after examination; failure to pass the test; refusal to take, use or agree to

When our son was six, he brought in a planter full of dirt so he could water the plant. I protested and told him there was no plant. He continued to water the dirt and insisted there was life in there. And I continued to shake my head and think what a good imagination he had. A week or so later a spindly little plant was standing proudly in the planter. Why hadn't I been able to see it?

So many people are like that plant. They are there with something to give to humanity and the Kingdom of God, but nobody seems to notice their worth. We look at them and see no real potential there. Then, someone comes along who sees something more than a pot of dirt. They take the time to care for them and nurture them and a beautiful plant emerges. I wonder how many plants there are around us that we can't see?

Maybe you are one of those plants. All you need is for someone to see the real you, who you are down deep. If someone would just spend a little time watering what looks like a pot of dirt, you know the seed would grow. You know there is a seed in your heart and you are not alone in that knowledge. God knows, too! He sees the potential in every one of us, and He will till the soil in our lives if we just won't quit. He wants to nurture us and help us become all He has designed us to be.

John Mark was a young man who was rejected by the great apostle Paul after he failed the test on their missionary journey. But that was not the end of his ministry, because someone saw the seed in that pot of dirt and took the time to cultivate it into a strong plant.

****

John Mark is spoken of in the Scripture by several names – John Mark, John, Mark and Marcus. The meanings of his names are very interesting, especially considering his story. John means "Jehovah has been gracious". Mark means "a large hammer".

A hammer is an instrument to be used to accomplish something. In the hand of an angry man, it can inflict wounds or be used to vandalize someone's property. When used by an inexperienced person, the results may be acceptable but less than artful. And in the hands of an immature child, there can be unforeseen danger. But in the hand of an experienced carpenter, it can accomplish beautiful work that will last down through the years.

As we walk along with John Mark through his life, we will see how relevant those names are. He was a young man ready to learn, but made a mistake that could have cost him the realization of his calling. But God. For those who are eager to learn, God always provides a teacher. Surely, Jehovah was gracious to John Mark.

There are three main players in John Mark's story as recorded in the Bible – Paul, Barnabus and, of course, John Mark. We have already met Paul.

In Colossians 4:10 we learn that Barnabus was John Mark's uncle. Mary, John Mark's mother, was a sister to Barnabus. It was in her house that the believers met to pray for Peter's release when he was in prison. When their prayers were answered and Peter was released, he came to her house with a remarkable praise report.

Barnabus was called "the son of consolation". Consolation means to comfort or to cheer a person up in the time of a loss. When you get to know him, you understand how he got that title. Barnabus accepted Paul when the other disciples were still skeptical of his conversion story. They didn't trust the 'persecutor turned disciple', but Barnabus took Paul to the apostles and told them how he had preached boldly about Jesus in Damascus.

We all need a friend like that at some time or another in our lives. One who sees into our heart and gives us the opportunity to grow and gain experience. One who sees us when we seem to be invisible to others and who stands with us so we won't have to stand alone.

Later, Barnabus went to Antioch to preach and a great revival was the result. He left that successful revival long enough to find Paul and bring him back so he could minister with him in Antioch. They stayed there about a year teaching the people.

Barnabus wasn't afraid that he would be "upstaged" by Paul's ministry. He must have sensed a need to have Paul work alongside him and he wasn't apprehensive about who might get the credit. Barnabus was obviously more interested in seeking God's purpose than in collecting trophies for his accomplishments. God can trust people like Barnabus because they seek the will of God with a pure heart. They have a servant's heart rather than striving to climb the ladder of success and to be great.

So, now we have Paul and Barnabus as a team in ministry. They left Antioch to take relief to their Christian brothers in Judea who were experiencing a famine. When they left Judea to return to Antioch, they took John Mark with them. Soon after that, Barnabus, Paul and the other prophets and teachers in Antioch were fasting and praying when the Holy Ghost spoke to them to send Barnabus and Paul out to do the work He had called them to do. When they went on this missionary journey, they took John Mark along as their assistant. What an open door for this young man! He was travelling with seasoned men of God. Not many had that privilege. It was a wonderful opportunity for him to grow in his walk with Christ and in ministry.

When they had travelled from Seleucia, Cyprus, Salamis, Paphos, Perga and Pamphylia, the Scripture says, "and John departing from them returned to Jerusalem." No reason given. No explanation. John Mark suddenly left his ministry with Barnabus and Paul and went back home. Period.

After the two missionaries completed their journey (without John Mark), they went back to Jerusalem to settle some doctrinal questions. Judas Barsabas and Silas went back to Antioch with them to deliver the ruling, and Silas decided to stay there with them.

They ministered in Antioch for an undisclosed amount of time, "Paul said to Barnabas, "Let us now go back and visit our brethren in every city where we have preached the word of the Lord, and see how they are doing." Barnabus was willing and wanted to take John Mark with them. Paul didn't think it was good to take him since he had deserted them in Pamphylia on the last trip. Their disagreement was so severe that Paul and Barnabus separated after all that time in ministry together.

Paul chose Silas to go with him. It was on this trip that Paul met Timothy whom he would later call his son in the faith. God had a young man for Paul to train, but it wasn't John Mark. However, that did not mean John Mark had no place in God's Kingdom. It simply meant his place was somewhere else and with someone else.

Barnabus took John Mark with him and sailed to Cyprus. He was just the person to train this young man and give him the opportunity to mature in the Lord and in service. Perhaps God knew he was not ready to face what Paul would face. Paul's dangerous, controversial and zealous ministry may not have been conducive to John Mark's gifting. Who knows the reason!

Can you imagine how John Mark must have felt after being rejected by the great Apostle Paul? He probably thought, "Paul's right; I don't deserve to go. I'm a failure because I deserted before. Paul doesn't have any faith in me because I am useless."

Think of it. It is one thing to be rejected by someone, but another thing altogether when we know we have done something that caused them to reject us. When that happens, guilt washes over us and Satan's accusations begin to swirl through our heads. He passes judgment and condemns us leaving us without hope. So we come to the conclusion we might as well quit. Yet, Jesus calls us to Himself. He convicts us (calls our attention to the problem), shows us how to make it right and leads us out. We may fail a test here and there, but there is no reason to quit following Jesus, because He will not reject us. If we turn to Him, He will put us back on the right path.

Sometimes it's hard for us to realize that one season of our life has ended and God is setting us in a new direction. Rather than seeing it as the next step in our journey, we feel we have failed and God has resorted to Plan B for our lives. That is usually not the case. It probably means we need more training. Or it could be God wants to simply move us to another area of ministry. Each season of life has its purpose in preparing us to go deeper in our relationship with Jesus and to surrender everything to Him.

There have been times in my life when a door opened that seemed like a dream. I couldn't imagine that it would have ever opened to me, but for some reason, nothing would come of it. It seemed the door opened then closed almost immediately. It was an "almost" opportunity that seemingly had no purpose. It rose up and then faded away. I've often wondered what could have been 'if' this or 'if' that, but God chose another way, and He did it for a purpose that only He knew. Nothing is happenstance when we are led by the Holy Spirit.

Why did John Mark's "big break" fall apart? I don't know, but I suspect he needed to grow a little more. His stint with Paul and Barnabus was all part of the maturing process. Sometimes we learn more from our mistakes and failures than from our successes.

We can read in the Bible extensively about the travels of Paul and Silas. But what happened to Barnabus and John Mark on their journey? The Scripture doesn't follow their travels, so we don't know the details of their ministry. But John Mark obviously grew under Barnabus' mentoring.

God had a man of faith in John Mark's life willing to give him another chance. Barnabus still believed in him. He saw a seed that needed water and some sunlight. He saw a young man who needed to grow in the Word and the power of the Spirit. Now we can see clearly why Barnabus was called the "son of consolation". Just as he gave Paul a chance, he was willing to nurture John Mark.

Every child of God has their place in His Kingdom. We are all different parts in the Body of Christ that function in various ways but are equally important. Think about the parts of our bodies. If you had to give up a part of your body, which would you chose? Would you want to give up your heart or your brain? Your foot or your hand? We don't want to lose any part because they are all important to the way we live our lives.

God had gifted John Mark, too. But his gift needed some experience and guidance before he could be fully useful to God. It wasn't enough to be able to hammer a nail with a little bend to it. It wasn't acceptable to use the gift in an inexperienced way that could endanger others or himself. He needed to develop that gift under the Spirit's direction as God intended.

John Mark was blessed (as we all are) that "Jehovah is gracious". God's grace is His Spirit's influence on our hearts and its reflection in our lives. John Mark was changed by this wonderful grace of God within him to accomplish beautiful, Spirit-led work in God's kingdom. He received the training and experience he needed and was fully functioning in the Body of Christ.

John Mark became beneficial for many people – even the Apostle Paul. I love how these little clips about John Mark are included in the Scripture. In a letter to the Colossians, Paul told them if John Mark came to them, they were to receive him. In writing to Timothy, he said, "Get Mark and bring him with you, for he is useful to me for ministry." In his letter to Philemon, Paul includes Mark in his list of fellow laborers he wishes Philemon to greet for him.

At some point, Mark was Peter's companion. Peter wrote, "She who is in Babylon, elect together with you, greets you; and so does Mark my son." You have probably read Mark's writings, too. He authored the gospel that bears his name. Peter was most likely the one God used to help supply him with his firsthand information, and the Holy Spirit supplied him with the inspiration.

After the big dispute between Barnabus and Paul about John Mark, it could have been grounds for him to quit. Instead, it was a turning point in the right direction.

When I graduated from high school, I had to write a speech to deliver during the ceremony. I wrote what I considered to be a great inspirational speech, but the head of the English Department told me it sounded like I was preaching a sermon – REWRITE IT! I handled the rejection well. I went to my English teacher, cried and shared my despair and doom with her. I had worked hard! There was nothing left to do! She must have seen the seed buried there, because she gently began to help and encourage me. After my speech was given during the graduation ceremony, the head of the English Department told my teacher that my speech was the best one given. Rather than quitting, sometimes we need to simply regroup and carry on.

It is so easy to feel like giving up when we work hard and still don't make it. But there is always hope. The Holy Spirit will be there to comfort you and urge you on. If you feel like quitting – DON'T! This is not the end. It is a turning point. It is a season of learning. Keep following the leadership of the Holy Spirit.

Maybe you feel like a little seed underneath a lot of dirt. It may seem you will never see the light of day, and you have lost hope. Allow the Word of God to feed you and the Spirit of God to refresh you with living water. You will live again!

Or maybe you feel like a hammer that causes destruction every time you try to use it. You feel like a failure and the enemy has shown you every reason why you might as well stop trying. Don't listen to him. Listen to Jesus and allow the Master Carpenter to show you the right way to swing a hammer. That is when you will start making real progress.

****

WHAT ABOUT ME?

Once we recognize what God has placed in our hands to use for His Kingdom, we need to allow Him to place His hand over ours. If we try on our own, we won't accomplish much. But with the training the Lord provides and by His Holy Spirit we will get the job done perfectly.

"Therefore do not cast away your confidence, which has great reward. For you have need of endurance, so that after you have done the will of God, you may receive the promise." Hebrews 10:35-36

Am I being overlooked by others? In what ways?

Can I look back at the direction of my life and clearly see the wisdom in each step of the path God has chosen for me?

Am I willing to be taught? Am I willing to surrender to the will of God?

Is it possible I am overlooking someone who is in need of a little tender loving care?

> **WORD STUDY**
>
> Cast – throw away, lose
>
> Confidence – assurance, conviction
>
> Reward – reimbursement or compensation
>
> Endurance – constancy, patience

Chapter Five

ACCEPTANCE - JESUS

> **ACCEPT**
> to receive willingly, to approve or agree with, to be pleased with or believe in.

When I went into my email inbox, I noticed the subject line on two of the emails that contrasted drastically. One said, "Thank you for being loyal" and the other said, "how rude". What conflicting opinions! The 'loyal' message was from an office supply store that I frequented. The 'how rude' message was from my sister who was pretending to be indignant with me for not emailing her for two days.

As Christians, we will always have to face conflicting opinions about who we are. Some people will praise us and be in total agreement with us while others are critics. And, unlike my sister's joking, these critics can be very serious and harsh, even belligerent at times. We just need to keep standing on the Truth – Jesus Christ.

Jesus always seemed to have drastically conflicting opinions about Who He was, what He did and what He taught. Some people loved Jesus and others hated Him. Some received His teachings while others were enraged by them and opposed everything He said and did. But Jesus did not let any of it sway Him from His purpose or take away from the fact of Who He is.

****

We are more familiar with the persecution Jesus endured rather than the acceptance He received, and rightly so. The rejection, persecution and suffering of Jesus was necessary so our salvation could be purchased with His blood. But there were times when He was actually accepted by the people, and the multitudes believed in Him. He knew He had to handle that acceptance with great care if he was to stay in tune with the Father. He never let rejection or acceptance change Him, His actions, or His message. He knew Who He was, that His works were of God and His message was true. So, He stood firm, regardless of the opinions of the world. Jesus Christ never changes!

We have seen that rejection can be an obstacle to our Christian journey, but most of us are not as aware of the dangers of acceptance. Acceptance is probably one of the most subtle threats to our walk with God. The temptation to turn from God's path does not always come through discouragement or negative circumstances. It can come though excitement and smooth sailing. When it seems things are finally "going our way", we need to be careful. "Our way" usually isn't God's way.

The danger of acceptance is almost imperceptible because it offers circumstances that seem so perfect and comfortable. We may have a group of people who are supporting us and pressing us onward. We miss the danger because it is not a hostile takeover. In fact, they are well-meaning people but are not wholly following the voice of the Holy Spirit. But because of the seemingly perfect circumstances, we slowly begin to let down our guard and rest in the false peace of our acceptance instead of the peace of God. But circumstances change. So, before long, we are far away from God and our circumstances are far from peaceful.

Jesus' presence among the people and His availability to them was probably one thing that invited the crowds. He was one of them. He actually walked among them. Emanuel, God with us. Can you imagine the religious rulers of His day making themselves accessible to the common folks? They were far removed from the masses and were an elite company that considered themselves to be on a much higher plane than the commoners and worthy to be esteemed by them. But Jesus spoke to the people individually and touched them, even those with leprosy. It was evident that He cared for them and had true compassion.

His teachings were not like those of the scribes and Pharisees, either. He spoke with an authority they didn't possess. Then, there were the miracles. He cast out devils, healed the sick, opened blinded eyes and deaf ears. He even raised the dead. So, the crowds traveled for miles to get to Jesus. Zachaeus, a rich tax collector, even climbed a tree to catch of glimpse of Him. Jesus was everything the Jewish leaders were not. He was genuine. He was powerful. He was kind. He was bold. He had wisdom like they had never heard before. So, their expectations grew and they could only come to one conclusion. Jesus was the Messiah they had been waiting for. The One their ancestors had waited for. Surely He would free them from Roman rule and set up His kingdom in Jerusalem. Even His disciples thought He had come to set up an earthly kingdom.

So, Jesus was accepted, but for many of the wrong reasons. He couldn't commit Himself to these people, because what they expected of Him was not what He was sent to do. His whole purpose was to do what the Father told Him to do and to say what the Father told Him to say. He knew their acceptance would turn to disillusionment and anger when they realized that. They would turn from Him as quickly as they had turned to Him.

If we consider the pressure that elevated position of honor would place on a person, it seems a pretty heady place to be. People flocking to hear us speak and receive a miracle. Everybody wanting to touch us or just see us in person. There are those who take advantage of that situation and use it for their own glory. It would be so easy to fall into that trap. When that happens, it is a snare to the followers and to the soul of the one who allowed their focus to be turned from Jesus by the praise of the people.

Leaders of churches and other ministries (large and small) are often put on a pedestal by their followers. After awhile, they get accustomed to being in a place of honor, everyone wanting an audience with them and everyone singing their praises. It would be difficult not to allow pride to slip in along with a feeling of being above others. It would be easy to start believing in yourself instead of the God Who is using you. Pride leads to an independent, haughty spirit, and it has caused many to fall. An independent spirit causes us to disconnect from Jesus rather than depending on Him. When we reach that point, we lose the anointing and power that comes from His Holy Spirit.

If we get too used to the acceptance of people, we will find it difficult to follow God when He tells us to do something we know will go against public opinion. We will find it difficult to speak the truth of God's Word when it is not acceptable to the people. We won't be willing to let go of our status to do the will of the Father.

The humanity of Jesus offered many opportunities for Him to get caught up in the will of the people as they thronged Him, believed on Him and praised Him. But He never committed Himself to anyone but the Father. Jesus had a spirit of meekness. He had power to do anything He wanted to do, but He only wanted to do the will of the Father. Just because we have the power to do something, it doesn't mean we should do it.

Jesus had to constantly be discerning and cautious. He had to stay connected to the Father's will and not give in to His humanity. It's not to say God doesn't send good things our way. Surely He does.

And He blesses us with people who support us and share our vision for ministry. But He knows our ego tends to grow in times of abundance. And we don't sense our need for Him in those times. Jesus had to walk the balance of ministering to the people He came to die for and obeying the will of the Father. So do we.

As soon as Jesus came up from the waters of baptism, a dove descended and the Father's voice was heard saying, "This is my beloved Son in Whom I am well pleased." (KJV) Immediately after that He was led into the wilderness to be tempted of the devil. Did Satan tempt Him by trying to intimidate Him or persecute Him? No. He tried to get Him to join forces with him and reach His goal of glory by another method. But Jesus would have to abandon His mission to redeem us in order to accept Satan's terms. He would have to stop following what the Father told Him to do. He knew exactly how to accomplish the mission of our redemption and receive glory. So, He rejected Satan's offers. He was determined to accomplish the will of the Father the Father's way.

Jesus took on Himself human flesh, so the devil appealed to that flesh. "The Word (Jesus) became flesh and dwelt among us." The temptations Satan used with Jesus in the wilderness fall into the categories mentioned in 1 John 2:16. "For all that is in the world, the lust of the flesh, and the lust of the eyes, and the pride of life, is not of the Father, but is of the world." Lust is a craving, a desire for what is forbidden (the exact opposite of our love and desire for God). It comes from our flesh which is our earthy nature apart from and opposed to God. Our flesh will lead us away from God. This passage of Scripture refers to the eyes as an instrument misused by our flesh to lure us toward evil desires. Our vision can provide an avenue for temptation causing us to fall into sin.

When Satan showed Jesus the splendor he promised to give Him, he was trying to appeal to the flesh that Jesus had taken on Himself. It didn't work. Jesus would not make a deal with the devil.

The pride of life is another facet of the flesh. It tends to boast and is arrogant. It is that part of us that says "I can trust in my own power and resources; I can handle it." Pride trusts in the stability of earthly things and human power…the things that will not last. It is the opposite of a spirit of meekness that depends on God. Meekness is power under God's control. It is our obedience to and dependence on God. When we follow after the things of this world, we exchange the glory of God for the temporary glory of this world.

Jesus knew the danger of these areas of temptation. The only way to conquer them was to stay connected to the Father. That is also the only way we can avoid falling in times of temptation. Satan appeals to our flesh, but our spirit must surrender to the will of God.

Satan knows if he can simply keep us away from God, we will lose our power, identity and possessions in Christ. Jesus understood His union with the Father was the key to the success of His mission. We need to have that same understanding. If Satan can keep us busy with good activities, we won't have time to hear from God and accomplish His mission.

Let's look at a few instances when the crowd was following Jesus. The first one is found in John 2:23-25. "Now when He was in Jerusalem at the Passover, in the feast day, many believed in His name, when they saw the miracles which He did. But Jesus did not commit Himself unto them, because He knew all men, and needed not that any should testify of man: for He knew what was in man."

The words 'believed' and 'commit' come from the same Greek word. It means to have faith in something or someone to the point of entrusting oneself to them. The people believed. They were trusting in Jesus. They were ready to follow Him. But He knew He could not afford to commit to them. He understood fully the volatility and instability of mankind. He knew they were only looking for temporal blessings and were still spiritually blind. They didn't understand the whole concept of Who He was and what He was sent to do. He knew when they found out, they would reject Him.

After Jesus fed a crowd of 5,000 men plus women and children with only five loaves of bread and two fish, the crowd was ready to crown Him as their king. "Then those men, when they had seen the sign that Jesus did, said, "This is truly the Prophet who is to come into the world." Therefore, when Jesus perceived that they were about to come and take Him by force to make Him king, He departed again to the mountain by Himself alone." (John 6:14-15)

Here again, the people were believing that Jesus was the prophet they had been waiting for. He was destined to be their king, but not this way. He was not destined to be an earthly king, because He is the King of all kings, not just the King of Israel! If He gave in to the will of the people, He would relegate His true, rightful position, and we would still be lost.

Notice how Jesus responded. He went to be alone with the Father. That is how we recover our perspective and reestablish our purpose. Listening to the crowd can be overwhelming and confusing. Just because a situation appears to be a good thing, it isn't necessarily the right way to go. We need to know if it is God opening the door or if it is a trap turning us from God's best. When we pull away and seek God, we will hear the voice of the Holy Spirit speaking truth to our spirit.

How many times have we had an offer that was life changing? It miraculously appeared out of nowhere. Suddenly, it seemed that our moment had arrived. Our mind and emotions were riding high. But deep in our spirit, we sensed something was not right. Then we know. It is a good opportunity, but it is not God's opportunity for us. That is the time to run to the Father and re-establish our "oneness" with Him just like Jesus did.

Another time when the crowd was accepting Jesus was when He rode into Jerusalem on a donkey. That may seem very humbling to us, but the donkey was symbolically the ride of kings in those days. All of Jerusalem was gearing up for the feast of the Passover. The crowd was at an all-time high. Then Jesus entered the city. The excitement was palpable. The crowds saw their king approaching and their expectations of His kingdom in Jerusalem appeared to be coming to pass. They were so full of joy and making so much noise in their praise and celebration of Jesus' arrival, that the religious rulers became angrier than ever before.

What would our thoughts be in that situation? If a crowd was that excited to see us riding into town? Our thoughts might go something like this: "I can't turn this down. Just look at the crowds! They believe in me. They need me, and I can't let them down. Look at them! They are so eager and hopeful to see the kingdom of God and so anxious to be set free."

If Jesus had entertained those thoughts and given in to the people's immediate need, the redemption of our souls would not be possible. Jesus had to keep His focus on the goal and His eyes on the Father. He looked into the future at all the souls who would be redeemed, and also to taking His seat beside the Father. "Jesus, the author and finisher of our faith, who for the joy that was set before Him endured the cross, despising the shame, and has sat down at the right hand of the throne of God." (Hebrews 12:2)

Jesus knew the outcome of His purpose. It would bring joy to Him, to the Father, and to billions of souls who would reap the benefits of His death and resurrection. He looked beyond the present to the future. He looked beyond the immediate to the eternal.

It is hard to let people think we have let them down because they don't understand our reasons for following the voice of the Spirit. It is hard to see them hurt or angry at us. But we have to do the will of the Father so we can reach the higher goal He has called us to.

I knew a man who was called to ministry, but by his own admission, was not called to pastor. He became involved with a group of people who needed a pastor, and they asked him to fill that position. At first, he said 'no'. It wasn't his calling. But something inside him stood up when he realized he loved the people and wanted to protect them by meeting their need. So, he agreed to be their pastor. It was short-lived, and the people were right back where they started from before long.

Jesus knew the will of the Father and followed it faithfully, even when the crowd was disappointed and couldn't understand. Within the week, the same crowd who had ushered Jesus into Jerusalem in thunderous praise was just as emotional in their shouts to "Crucify Him." They had been accepting what they wanted from Him, but they didn't actually accept Him or His true mission. As soon as they found out He wasn't going to do things their way, they didn't just walk away, they turned violently against Him.

But that didn't stop Jesus from suffering for them and dying for them. It was His purpose. And He knew there was a glorious time coming when He would be seated at the right hand of the Father and many sons and daughters would be able to come into the kingdom because of His sacrifice.

****

WHAT ABOUT ME?

Turning away from a crowd who accepts us can be hard to do. The urgent often steals our attention away from what is really important and keeps us from carrying out the mission God has assigned to us. Beware of falling into the trap of acceptance and compromising your faith and calling. Acceptance can cause us to quit following God and not even realize it. Lay aside everything that keeps you from winning the race.

"Wherefore seeing we also are compassed about with so great a cloud of witnesses, let us lay aside every weight, and the sin which doth so easily beset us, and let us run with patience the race that is set before us, Looking unto Jesus the author and finisher of our faith; who for the joy that was set before him endured the cross, despising the shame, and is set down at the right hand of the throne of God.

For consider him that endured such contradiction of sinners against himself, lest ye be wearied and faint in your minds. Ye have not yet resisted unto blood, striving against sin." Hebrews 12:1-4 (KJV)

How have I allowed acceptance by others to deceive me and lead me away from God's calling?

What areas of my life are still not surrendered to Jesus?

What is weighing me down from accomplishing the mission Jesus has set before me?

Being completely honest with myself, am I following the will of my own flesh, the will of others, or the will of the Father?

Have I fallen into the snare of pride in "my work" for Jesus? Or am I a cleansed vessel allowing Him to flow through me?

> **WORD STUDY**
>
> Weight – burden, encumbrance
>
> Sin – violation of God's law
>
> Beset – to hinder in every direction
>
> Patience – steadfastness, endurance, constancy

Chapter Six

ENVY – THE PSALMISTS

> **ENVY**
> discontent, ill will and resentment over others' advantages, possessions, etc. – desire for something belonging to another.

My sister lives in Colorado. She sent me an email describing how she looked out her window one night and saw a deer standing on a beautiful snow-covered hill behind her house. It was illuminated by the soft light of the moon. She said there was a glow on the snow and the deer. Meanwhile, back in the Southeast, we were experiencing messy rain. So, I answered her essentially like this: "We don't have beautiful snow. We have RAIN! And the last deer I saw was dead on the side of the road. But all is not lost. We still have some magic moments, too. I just can't think of any right now."

Have you ever really felt that way? It seems nothing is going right for you, and everybody else is doing fine, especially those who you think deserve it less than you. But you know God is in control. You can't see Him at work, but you know He is, and that His wonders go far beyond even snow, moonlight and deer.

****

ASAPH

Asaph couldn't think of any magic moments, either. So he wrote his own version of Lamentations. The word lament is a kinder word for moaning, complaining and whining. Asaph turned his eyes in the wrong direction and almost lost his footing. In Psalm 73, he begins with a disclaimer for the views he was about to share at the beginning of his testimony. His disclaimer is in the form of a proclamation of the goodness of God that is extended to those who have a clean heart. Once he establishes that truth, he begins the story of how he got on the slippery slope of envy and almost fell. "But as for me, my feet were almost gone; my steps had well nigh slipped." (vs. 2 KJV) What caused him to slip and almost fall? He was envious when he saw that those who are wicked seemed to be safe, well, happy, healthy, peaceful and even prosperous.

Have you ever looked at the lives of those who live immoral lifestyles apart from God, and it seems they are blessed? They are openly ungodly, without shame and actively bad people, yet it seems everything works out for them. It is a snare to our souls when we begin to compare God's dealings in our lives with others, and when we try to figure it out in the natural instead of focusing on the spiritual.

Asaph wasn't so unlike the rest of us with the exception that he was actually daring enough to put his thoughts on paper. They were not fleeting thoughts, either. He obviously gave this matter serious consideration over a period of time. He goes into great detail about his observations. Think of this. Asaph's words made it into Holy Writ. For some reason, God chose for them to be preserved down through time for us to read. So, we must have something in common. And there must be something we can learn from his experience.

Asaph noticed these wicked people had no pain in death, their bodies were essentially healthy and strong, and they didn't endure struggles and hard work like others. Neither did they seem to have problems constantly striking against them.

They wore their pride openly like one would wear a pricey chain around their neck. They didn't even try to hide their arrogance. Yet here they were in good health and had more of this world's goods than you could imagine. Worse still, they didn't earn their wealth from honest work, but by unjust gain. Yet, even their evil devices seemed to cover them like fine clothing, making them look prosperous and in control.

After all this, Asaph still has more observations to share. He goes on to register another complaint; their blessings are in direct contradiction to their open wickedness. And on top of everything else, they blaspheme. They speak evil of the heavens (the place of God's throne) and of God Himself. They speak evil of other people, even boasting of the harm they will do and threatening openly of oppressing and manipulating people. He says wherever they go, they make their presence known by their boasting. Even when they drink a cup of iniquity, no apparent harm comes to them. In contrast, the very evil they do makes them look good, powerful and confident as it hides what they really are. They seem invincible.

Psalm 94:7 focuses in a little clearer on these people that Asaph envies. "They say, "The Lord does not see; the God of Jacob takes no notice." Job knew about this type of people, too. He wrote that they say, "'What does God know? Can He judge through the deep darkness?" These people obviously believe they are invincible, so they act like it. They actually believe they are clever enough to deceive God and can hide their evil ways from Him.

Asaph's observation in a nutshell is found in verse 12. "Behold, these are the ungodly, Who are always at ease; They increase in riches." It is a skewed view of one who had "well nigh slipped." He considers them peaceful, secure and successful. God's viewpoint is much broader and more accurate.

In verses 13 and 14, we find out why Asaph's observations upset him so much. Here he gives us what his "discovery" means to him personally. "Surely I have cleansed my heart in vain, And washed my hands in innocence. For all day long I have been plagued, And chastened every morning." He says in essence, "I have lived a godly life, making myself pure in God's eyes. But it was all useless. I've only put myself through useless disciplines. They are empty and worthless. They bear no fruit and have no reward."

Asaph was at a very real danger point. Because of his envy, he was doubting God, blaming God and almost ready to quit. Yet, it was at this point in his deliberations that something changed. This is where the clouds of deceit gave way and the light of truth began to shine through. Suddenly, he tells us if he ends with that viewpoint and frame of mind, he would be deceitful to the generations to come. What changed his mind? The next verses explain it.

"When I thought how to understand this, It was too painful for me - Until I went into the sanctuary of God; Then I understood their end." It was painful for him. He was putting forth so much effort to try to understand and was wearing himself out mentally and emotionally. He was leading himself down a mental path that led to everything but truth. Then he went into the sanctuary.

The sanctuary is a consecrated place that is set apart to seek God, Who is Truth. There, in the presence of God, he was once again enlightened to the truth and realized the folly and foolishness of his earlier thoughts. Three words Asaph used in verse 12 should have made him pause, shake himself and review what 'seems to be' against what actually is. But possibly he was too far gone to see it anywhere but in the presence of God. The prosperity of the wicked was "in the world". Then it ended.

In the presence of God, the false claims of the world vanish like morning mist in the sun. The reality of what is genuinely important and lasting comes to the surface and we see the difference in real peace and this world's peace; eternal success and this world's success. God's presence clears our focus on reality and causes everything else to crumble into nothingness. Looking to Jesus gives us balance and truth. We can be assured that God's presence with us is worth far more than the passing wealth, fame and power of this life.

Suddenly, this thinker, this psalmist with a testimony, came to his senses and saw that his thoughts were just as foolish as the wickedness of the wicked man. In this world, the wicked seemed to live it up, but for eternity, they would be in darkness and destruction. "Oh, how they are brought to desolation, as in a moment! They are utterly consumed with terrors." He sees how quickly the landscape of their lives change. It may seem they are "blessed" for a long time, but it's really a short span of time compared to eternity. The change from security to destruction is so sudden that they are terrorized and alarmed by it. Their days of power, prestige, wealth, health, peace, and success are all over in the blink of an eye. They will never recover any of it. The time of judgment and justice will come for all evil and all good. Those who think themselves to be invincible will one day be brought into account before Almighty God.

Let's pause and take a little side trip here for a moment. God does not take pleasure in the demise of wicked people. He does, however, take pleasure in the demise of wickedness itself. The problem is that wickedness can only operate where there is a person who consents to practice it. It is God's desire for the wicked to turn and be saved, because sin will be judged and punished regardless who it is that has given it a place to lodge within them.

In Ezekiel 33:11, God tells Ezekiel to "Say to them: 'As I live,' says the Lord God, 'I have no pleasure in the death of the wicked, but that the wicked turn from his way and live. Turn, turn from your evil ways! For why should you die, O house of Israel?" This is a God who loves us with passion and compassion. He has spoken again and again to draw us to Himself and save us, but He will not reward sin or allow it in His presence. Sin cannot survive the holiness of God, neither can a body of flesh that houses evil stand in God's presence and live.

In this same chapter of Ezekiel, God declares that those who have followed Him, then turn aside and cease to follow Him, will not escape destruction. And those who have been wicked, yet turn from that wickedness, will be saved. His heart is to save, not destroy, but He cannot accept sin. It will be destroyed. Sadly, sin will take many people with it to destruction even though the blood of Jesus was shed to rid them of sin and bring them to salvation.

In John 3:16-17, we see the love and compassion of God in sending Jesus to us. "For God so loved the world, that he gave his only begotten Son, that whosoever believeth in him should not perish, but have everlasting life. For God sent not his Son into the world to condemn the world; but that the world through him might be saved." (KJV)

When Asaph realizes who has the real blessings, he realizes how ignorant he has been, not knowing or seeing the truth. He is convicted, pierced through his soul for his foolishness, and he grieves for thinking God could be unjust or that serving Him could be in vain. Through it all he realizes God has not left Him, but has brought Him back to reality in His presence. God walked with him through this whole confusing experience to guide him back to truth. And He would continue to guide him. Asaph needed to see into the realm of the Holy Spirit instead of the natural. We cannot depend on our flesh to speak truth to us. Only Jesus and His Word are truth, and Satan tries to blind us from that truth. We need the Spirit of God within us to help us see what is real. "But the natural man does not receive the things of the Spirit of God, for they are foolishness to him; nor can he know them, because they are spiritually discerned." 1 Corinthians 2:14

Our riches, wisdom, wealth, health, success and prosperity in the kingdom of God are not temporary, but everlasting. The wicked have their best life now, in this world. The godly have the presence of God with them now and all the best forever.

Toward the end of his narrative, Asaph had complained about being dogged with problems. We may as well face the fact that since Satan declared war against God, we are born into and live our lives on a battlefield. There is a war going on with very real battles. Just by essence of birth, we become part of the battle, and we must choose sides. Good or evil. God or Satan. Life or death. Victory or defeat. Heaven or hell. Those who choose God's side are attacked with problems and tribulations. That's what we are promised. Some of those problems may seem overwhelming. Others may seem insignificant, but they are like a dog nipping constantly at our heels trying to wear us down over the course of time. They are sent from the enemy to turn our attention away from that which is important - the kingdom of God.

Jesus said, "If the world hates you, you know that it hated Me before it hated you." (John 15:18) And Paul warned us, "Yes, and all who desire to live godly in Christ Jesus will suffer persecution." (2 Timothy 3:12) In the face of those warnings, we are also promised victory in the end and that God is fighting for us. We are not alone in the battle, and we are already assured of the outcome.

Those who choose Satan's side will be used and abused by him, then abandoned when they face certain defeat. The only "prosperity" they have will be whatever temporary success they experience in the fleeting moments of this life. And Satan uses that same prosperity to control them and keep them ensnared in the trap he has them in.

Asaph had also complained about being chastised. God loves us too much to let us be lazy, undisciplined children who stay immature and whiny. He is about the task of making spiritually mature men and women out of us; people who are persistent in their faith, bold in their testimony, discerning and wise, strong and faithful. His discipline will turn us into men and women who never compromise the truth, but are relentless in making it known at any cost. So, yes. Out of His love for His children He will chasten us to help us grow up strong, healthy and functional.

Asaph ends with this solid truth. "But it is good for me to draw near to God: I have put my trust in the Lord God, that I may declare all thy works." (Psalm 73:28 KJV)

DAVID

Another well-known psalmist also had something to say about envying the wicked. David wrote part of what he had learned on the subject in Psalm 37. He begins with this warning against going down the slippery slope that Asaph nearly fell into.

"Do not fret because of evildoers, Nor be envious of the workers of iniquity. For they shall soon be cut down like the grass, And wither as the green herb." (Psalm 37:1-2

Fretting and worry are close cousins, and they never accomplish anything of value. Those who fret stay in a continual state of unrest, worry and anxiety by consistently feeding their minds with fearful thoughts of things they cannot control. That practice is unhealthy and will turn us from God. God will deal with the evildoers in His own time. He is loving and patient, giving us all time to repent. We need to leave it in His hands and trust His wisdom.

David gives us the antidote for fretting about the workers of unrighteousness and being envious of those who are evil doers. I wonder if he, too, found the answer in the sanctuary of the Lord. Rather than allowing ourselves to be obsessed and stressed by the evildoers around us, he gives us some measures we can take to intentionally turn our attention to God. Just like Asaph, David had also learned to shift his focus from the seemingly unfairness of life to the God of life and truth. David gives us several words of wisdom to keep us off the fretting track and get us back on God's track.

The only way we can stand strong is to keep our focus on Jesus. Looking at those around us can dishearten us. "Be anxious for nothing, but in everything by prayer and supplication, with thanksgiving, let your requests be made known to God; and the peace of God, which surpasses all understanding, will guard your hearts and minds through Christ Jesus." (Philippians 4:6-7) Rather than allowing anxiety to overcome us, we can turn to Jesus through prayer, acknowledging and thanking Him for His blessings, and asking Him to meet our needs. That is where we will have our minds stabilized in the truth.

Psalm 37:3 tells us, "Trust in the Lord, and do good; Dwell in the land, and feed on His faithfulness." When we get to know who God is, we will learn to trust Him. We find out from personal experience that we can rely on His integrity without being disappointed. We can count on the fact that God will deal with us in justice and love. When situations arise in our lives that are bad, He will ultimately bring good out of it. When we learn to trust Him, we will do what is right, regardless of His dealings with us or others, because we have come to know He is a good Father.

Verse 4 says, "Delight yourself also in the Lord: and he shall give you the desires of your heart." This verse may seem like a blank check for us to fill in however we choose, but there is a condition. We must delight in the Lord. When our pleasure and satisfaction in life is in the Lord, we have become one with Him. His presence becomes our vital life source. Our will becomes His will. The things that grieve His heart will grieve our hearts. And the things that bring Him pleasure will bring us pleasure. When we come to that relationship with Christ, we can ask what we will and it will be done.

Verse 5 invites us to, "Commit your way to the Lord; trust also in him; and he shall bring it to pass." When we have learned to trust Him and delight in Him, we will be able to commit our course of life into His hands with confidence. The word 'commit' means to entrust something into the care of another. Many of us want to do everything ourselves because we don't trust someone else to do it the way we think it should be done. Committing our way to Jesus is surrendering our will and trusting that His way is best.

Verse 7 may be difficult for us in our busy world. "Rest in the Lord, and wait patiently for Him; Do not fret because of him who prospers in his way, Because of the man who brings wicked schemes to pass." When we think of rest, we usually think of a vacation. Aside from that, rest sounds like a wonderful luxury that few of us have much time for. But rest in the Lord is essential, and it is not temporary. It is leaning on Him and allowing Him to lead. Our job is to follow. He wants us to come to the point where we have freedom from the cares of this life because we are completely trusting in Him. He wants us to cease from our activity and performances and allow Him to work through us. Jesus calls us to come to Him and find rest for our souls (our mind, will and emotions). We feel a need to fight and get vengeance, but God says the battle is His and we can rest in His victory. When He tells us to put on His armor, He never says to fight. He says to stand in what He has already provided. The only offensive piece of armor is the Word of God. And He wants us to use it proficiently.

Let's look at one more verse in this psalm of David. "Cease from anger, and forsake wrath: Do not fret - it only causes harm." To cease simply means to stop! We are not to join in with the evildoers, but do what is right and good. Don't respond in anger. Don't allow wrath to swallow you up. Don't do evil to get even with someone. It is not our place, but God's place to vindicate us. As children of God, we are called to walk a higher road and with a higher standard.

Keeping our focus on Jesus will keep us off the slippery slope. Sometimes the moment of unbelief is the turning point of our lives to throw us wholeheartedly into serving God. But we cannot play games with God. I believe He is open for us to ask Him questions, but not to question Him, His omnipotence, His wisdom, His judgments. We must look to Him for the answers to have our hearts made strong in truth. If we look elsewhere, we will quit serving Him and lose our souls. Only in the presence of God will we find the way out of our doubts and into the light of His glorious truth.

Remember the method Satan used to cause Eve to sin? He questioned God's word. "Hath God said?" Then he questioned God's motives. He told Eve in essence that God was holding out on them. If they ate that forbidden fruit they would become as gods. Satan still uses that tactic, only in different circumstances. Don't let him deceive you. Don't believe his lies that contradict the truth of God's word.

Don't believe his lies that question God's love for you. Jesus paid the price for us to have the best, eternal life in His presence. Don't let Satan cheat you out of that. Don't quit. Keep your focus on what is true and good.

****

WHAT ABOUT ME?

Asaph said his "steps had well nigh slipped." He came close to giving up. Most of us at some point have a challenge of our faith, a time of testing as to what we believe. Few of us voice it. Asaph was brave enough to bring it out in the open and allow God to help him through it. God knows our hearts, and we can share everything with Him. In His presence we find answers to unanswerable questions, peace in the middle of a battle, and hope in hopeless situations. We can trust Him to establish us in truth.

"The steps of a good man are ordered by the Lord: and he delighteth in his way. Though he fall, he shall not be utterly cast down: for the Lord upholdeth him with his hand." Psalm 37:23-24 (KJV)

What doubts have I entertained in my mind that have placed me on a slippery slope?

Have I talked to God about my doubts, or do I feel guilty and try to keep them suppressed?

How has Satan used my questions to try to turn me against God's Word?

Am I willing to take my questions/complaints into the "sanctuary" and deal with them once and for all?

What are some steps I can take to strengthen my trust in God?

WORD STUDY

Ordered – directed, established

Delighteth – to be pleased with

Utterly – completely, totally, without reversal

Upholdeth – supports, sustains, revives, refreshes

Hand – strength, power

Chapter Seven

CIRCUMSTANCES – BARTIMAEUS, THE BLIND MAN

> **CIRCUMSTANCES**
> the outward conditions affecting a person or situation; state of affairs

My husband is rather a jack-of-all-trades. He can take most broken things and make them useful again with a little time and effort (along with a few parts added). Most people would throw away some of those broken things, but not at my house! It gets the royal treatment and then returns to its duties.

There are many people who wind up with broken lives, sometimes lives that are shattered into pieces. I know Someone Who doesn't want those broken lives thrown away. He wants to take the time and effort to restore them, to give them something they thought they could never have. He wants to put new parts where the old ones are damaged or destroyed. Jesus not only can restore broken lives to usefulness, He is also willing to do it. Maybe you need restoration in your life. If so, call on the name of Jesus. He will fix what is broken in you so you can be very useful in His Kingdom. Yes, even you!

We need to cultivate the faith and ability to rise above our present conditions even when everyone around us tells us it's impossible and we need to just accept things as they are. They may be well-meaning, but our faith in people must take a back seat to our faith in God. And He says all things are possible to those who believe.

"Blind Bartimaeus" is a perfect example of a man who resisted public opinion to overcome his circumstances. He received healing and deliverance from a restrictive and oppressive life through faith in Jesus Christ. Although his identity was linked with his circumstances, that was about to change. We find his story in Mark 10.

****

Bartimaeus was the son of Timaeus. The name means "highly prized", but Bartimaeus probably didn't feel very prized. He was blind and unable to work to support himself. In those days there were no equal opportunity employers, occupational therapy classes or special training for those with a disability to learn a trade. So, he was doing the very thing that was expected of someone in his circumstances. He was sitting beside a public highway begging. He wasn't going anywhere on that highway. He was just sitting there hoping to collect some money from the people who were going somewhere. It would have been a decently busy highway since it was close to Jericho, and that is probably why he chose to make it his custom to sit in that particular spot to beg.

On this particular day, Jesus and His disciples were on that highway coming out of Jericho with a large crowd following them. Undoubtedly, Bartimaeus could heard the crowd. The bigger the crowd, the better the chance he had to make money. Then he heard that it was Jesus passing by. He must have felt a spark of hope for something more than a few coins. Maybe, just maybe, he could have a whole new life. Surely he had heard the stories of Jesus' miracles. Why not for him? So, he did the only thing he could. He began to "cry out". Those words mean to shriek or to scream. Bartimaeus meant business. He couldn't run through the crowd to search for Jesus, so he began to cry out in earnest, "Jesus, Son of David, have mercy on me!" He cried out for compassion from the miracle worker.

There were many in that crowd who definitely did not have compassion for the blind man who was desperate to get Jesus' attention. The Scripture tells us "many warned him to be quiet". His noise was a nuisance to them and they told him to stop yelling. Maybe they wanted Jesus' attention and they thought he would take their place. Maybe they thought he wasn't worthy for the Master to be bothered. We are not told why they tried to silence him, but it did not deter him at all. He refused to quit. Many would have said, "Oh, well, maybe they are right. Maybe it is useless to be screaming out in such a large crowd. I may as well give up." But no! Not "blind Bartimaeus"! His hope and faith had risen and he was determined. He didn't care what the crowd thought of him or how ridiculous his behavior may appear. Although the crowd told him to be quiet, "he cried the more a great deal." I love that phrase! That spark of hope had burst into a flame, and Bartimaeus would not be denied!

When people tell us just to accept things as they are, that there is no way God can restore our families, heal our hearts and bodies, renew our minds, deliver us from habits and sins, open doors and fulfill visions He has placed in our hearts, don't listen! They are wrong. When it looks like they are right, cry out to Jesus the more a great deal.

After telling us Bartimaeus kept crying out to Jesus, the next words in this account are priceless. "And Jesus stood still, and commanded him to be called. And they called the blind man, saying to him, 'Be of good comfort, rise; he is calling you." Suddenly, the crowd's message changed. Instead of berating him, now they were speaking kind words of encouragement. They were telling him to be comforted and come to Jesus. What a change! Jesus proved to the crowd that it was not futile for Bartimaeus to cry out. It made all the difference in the world. Instead of Bartimaeus giving up, the crowd gave in to the words of Jesus. They had to confess that Jesus was really asking him to come to Him. They saw that his cries had been answered and he had Jesus' full attention.

Jesus singled Bartimaeus out of that huge crowd. He called him out individually. I assure you today, Jesus knows your circumstances and He knows your name. He knows your heart. When you sincerely cry out to Him, He will hear you. Just as surely as Bartimaeus cried out specifically for Jesus, and Jesus called out specifically for Bartimaeus to come to Him. He loves you just the same.

When Bartimaeus heard Jesus' words, he cast "away his garment, rose, and came to Jesus." Bartimaeus threw off his beggar's cloak in faith even before he was healed. He was ready to be a new man. He was tired of wearing a beggar's cloak. He was tired of being blind, and he was ready for something new.

Jesus is still in the business of making us new. But we have to take off the old to prepare for the new. We can lay aside the old cloak that labels us as spiritually blind, sinful and unrighteous. We can become a new creation in Christ, exchanging our old sin-stained robe for His robe of righteousness.

Ephesians 4:22-24 speaks of putting off the old to make room for the new once we come to Jesus. "...that you put off, concerning your former conduct, the old man which grows corrupt according to the deceitful lusts, and be renewed in the spirit of your mind, and that you put on the new man which was created according to God, in true righteousness and holiness."

When Bartimaeus stood before Jesus, Jesus asked him a strange question. He said, "What do you want Me to do for you?" It seems what he needed was obvious enough, yet Jesus asked what he wanted Him to do. Sometimes we lack spiritual insight. Of course, it's obvious to Jesus what we need, but we often don't recognize the root of our problem. So, we ask for temporary things for a temporary fix. Many cry out to Jesus for a new life, but don't realize the root of the problem blocking them from that life is the sin that separates them from God. So they don't confess their sins and repent of them (turning away from them). When we ask Jesus to forgive our sins and cleanse us, we are on the right road.

Bartimaeus could have asked for enough money so he wouldn't have to beg. He could have asked for servants to help him live comfortably through life as a blind man. But Bartimaeus knew the root of the problem. And he immediately answered, "Lord, that I might receive my sight." That's all it took. Jesus said "Go your way; your faith has made you well. And immediately he received his sight, and followed Jesus in the way."

Because Bartimaeus had faith in Jesus, he received his miracle. His faith caused him to act, to step out and do something, so his circumstances were completely changed as a result. What did he do with his new set of circumstances? He followed Jesus in the way. His use of the highway had changed. It was no longer his destination to set up shop. Now it was the path he walked on as he followed Jesus. The story of Bartimaeus as we read it in Mark 10 begins with him on the highway as a beggar and ends with him on the highway as a child of God, following Jesus Christ.

Bartimaeus is a wonderful example of not quitting and calling out to Jesus in our circumstances. How can we learn from his example? We can consider the steps Bartimaeus took to arrive at the realization of his miracle. We can take those steps too.

The first thing that set Bartimaeus on the right path was to believe Jesus could heal him. He believed enough to act on it. His faith caused him to cry out to Jesus. Too often we turn to worry and trying to figure out our problems, or we may get our advice from counselors or other people we trust in. But Jesus is the "Wonderful Counselor". Many others have cried out to Jesus with the same results as Bartimaeus. In Psalm 34:4 David wrote, "I sought the Lord, and He heard me, and delivered me from all my fears." Jesus should be our first thought and our certain hope when we need help. When we cry out to Jesus in faith, He hears our cry and will turn our blindness to light. He can open our spiritual eyes to see the truth and enlighten us to know the solution for our dilemma. He can walk us through the process of changing our circumstances by the power of the Holy Spirit within us.

When, Bartimaeus heard that Jesus was calling Him to come to Him, he knew his next step was to get up and go to Jesus. It was as simple as that. Jesus had called for him to come, but Bartimaeus had to make the effort to go to Jesus.

How far are we willing to go to get in the presence of Jesus? All through Scripture, we see where God is seeking out mankind to come to Him. Jesus called us to come to Him and find rest. The Spirit of God speaking to our spirits calls us, but the choice is ours whether or not we will go to Him. Only those who take the step of answering Jesus' call to come to Him will find the rest He promises.

Bartimaeus had not received his sight at this point, but he was sure he would, sure enough to throw off his beggar's cloak. He rose up, casting aside the bondage of the past. He was focused on the things ahead of him, and he was putting off the things that identified him with his past as a blind beggar. Those days were over and a new day was dawning in his life. He believed it! Jesus was calling for him!

Bartimaeus was "forgetting those things which are behind and reaching forward to those things which are ahead". When we come to Christ, we can lay aside everything that identifies us with our past as a spiritually blind sinner, one who begs at the mercy of other people. We can know Jesus personally and walk with Him daily. Laying aside the sins of our past will draw us ever closer to Christ.

Colossians 3:8-10 tells us, "But now you yourselves are to put off all these: anger, wrath, malice, blasphemy, filthy language out of your mouth. Do not lie to one another, since you have put off the old man with his deeds, and have put on the new man who is renewed in knowledge according to the image of Him who created him." When we go to Jesus, we will not want any of those things to remain in our lives.

Before Bartimaeus knew it, he was standing in front of Jesus and Jesus was asking him what He wanted Him to do for him. As we have seen, he didn't hesitate. He wanted to have his sight. And he made his petition to Jesus, fully expecting to receive it. As children of God, we are told we can make our petitions known. "Let us therefore come boldly to the throne of grace that we may obtain mercy and find grace to help in time of need." (Hebrews 4:16)

It seems reasonable to assume that Bartimaeus' first glimpse out of his healed eyes was the face of Jesus! What a glorious thought. We need to consistently look into Jesus' face and see His glory and love. We can live in His presence every day. That is almost inconceivable, but we really can know Jesus on a personal level.

When we come to Jesus, we become a new creation. Our circumstances change because our heart has changed. Colossians 3:1-3 says, "If then you were raised with Christ, seek those things which are above, where Christ is, sitting at the right hand of God. Set your mind on things above, not on things on the earth. For you died, and your life is hidden with Christ in God."

From that point on, Bartimaeus walked in newness of life. Everything was different and He followed Jesus down the highway. Those who choose to follow Jesus leave behind this world and keep their focus on Him. If we don't stay close to Jesus, we will lose sight of Him and take the wrong path. But we do not have to be like those who turn off the path of eternal life. We can remain steadfast as new creatures in Christ Jesus. Our circumstances do not have to define who we are. Jesus can redefine us as children of the King! Jesus said, "Until now you have asked nothing in My name. Ask, and you will receive, that your joy may be full."

Don't be denied by the crowd telling you to be quiet. Instead be like Bartimaeus and "cry the more a great deal." Can't you hear Jesus calling for you?

****

WHAT ABOUT ME?

The advice of the crowd can cause us to give up on changing our circumstances, but Jesus knows how to give us a spiritual renovation that makes us profitable to Him. No one is worthless. No one is useless, not in the hands of the Master. Jesus wants to make us a new creation even more than we want it.

"For we ourselves were also once foolish, disobedient, deceived, serving various lusts and pleasures, living in malice and envy, hateful and hating one another. But when the kindness and the love of God our Savior toward man appeared, not by works of righteousness which we have done, but according to His mercy He saved us, through the washing of regeneration and renewing of the Holy Spirit, whom He poured out on us abundantly through Jesus Christ our Savior, that having been justified by His grace we should become heirs according to the hope of eternal life." Titus 3:3-7

"What circumstances in my life are weighing me down and keeping me from wholly following Jesus?

Are the voices of the crowd starting to discourage me?

Do I truly believe Jesus cares enough to "recycle" me into something profitable, even valuable?

Is my faith in Christ alone?

Do I believe Him enough to act on my faith?

> **WORD STUDY**
>
> Lust – longing for what is forbidden
>
> Malice – desire to injure or harm another
>
> Righteousness – in right standing with God
>
> Regeneration – spiritual rebirth; transformation
>
> Justified – made free of the guilt of sin
>
> Heir – one who receives something as set forth in a will

Chapter Eight

INJUSTICE – JOSEPH

INJUSTICE
an undeserved injury;
not being fair;
to be mistreated

We had an aloe plant that we left outside during the last cold snap of the winter and it died – we thought. We had not meant to mistreat it but were negligent of its care, and the part that survived turned brown except for a small tip that was still green. Aloe plants are wonderful for healing burns, so when I burned my hand, I broke off a part of that tip to soothe the pain. That little broken, mistreated aloe still provided healing for me. Surprisingly, with a little water and warmer weather, it sprang back to life. We are a little more careful with our aloe plant now. After all, it taught me a wonderful lesson.

Are we like that aloe plant? When we are mistreated, we can choose to dry up and become bitter; or we can be resilient and return good for evil. The latter changes hearts – ours and the offenders.

Joseph learned a valuable, albeit a hard-earned lesson, through years of injustice. His journey was long and difficult, but after all those trying years, God suddenly and miraculously turned night to a dazzling light of day.

****

Joseph was the next to the youngest child of Jacob, one of the patriarchs who was a descendant of Abraham. Joseph and his younger brother Benjamin were sons of Jacob's most beloved wife Rebekah. Joseph was favored by his father as well as by the Lord God Jehovah. His father gave him a coat of many colors that made his brothers jealous. And God gave him dreams that made them jealous. The dreams all had to do with Joseph's family bowing down to him. His brothers did not want to hear it. His father scolded him when he shared his dreams with him, yet he knew the favor of God was on Joseph. There were twelve brothers altogether.

The jealousy in Joseph's ten older brothers grew to a state of bitterness. That bitterness and resentment inside them finally caused them to instigate a plan to sell Joseph to some slave traders (human traffickers), sprinkle his beloved coat with goat's blood and tell their father that some wild animal must have eaten him. They brought Joseph's bloody coat to their father for a positive identification and to break the news of Joseph's "demise". When their father saw the bloody coat, he knew it was Joseph's, and he mourned the loss of his favored son.

It seems bad enough that the brothers hated Joseph enough to do such a thing to him. But they also knew what it would do to their father. Their hatred seemed to know no bounds.

Joseph's brothers had sold him to some Ishmaelites who took him to Egypt and sold him to Potiphar, the captain of Pharaoh's guard. So, Joseph wound up as a servant in Potiphar's house. It wasn't home, but Joseph seemed to have a good life there. The Bible tells us that, "The Lord was with Joseph, and he was a successful man." Potiphar saw that the favor of God was on Joseph and that he did all his service with excellence. So, he made Joseph overseer of his household and put him in authority over everything he had. That was pretty impressive for such a young man.

Before long, Potiphar's wife began trying to seduce Joseph and he refused her every time. So, she falsely accused Joseph of sexual assault, and Potiphar was so angry that he put him in the prison where the king's prisoners were taken. Joseph must have thought, "Not again! I was unjustly taken from my father's house and sold. And God brought good out of it. He gave me favor and raised me up and now this! How could this happen again?"

Isn't that like life? Just when we think everything is going the way we hoped it would, some injustice rips it from us. We start wondering if we just attract the wrong kind of people or if we are not meant to succeed at anything. But our thoughts and ways are not as high as God's thoughts and ways. He has something better. In Joseph's case, God had something that would be world-changing. Joseph had to be trained well to accomplish all that God had for him.

Once again, even in prison, "the Lord was with Joseph and showed him mercy, and He gave him favor in the sight of the keeper of the prison." Joseph was given authority over all the prisoners, "because the Lord was with him; and whatever he did, the Lord made it prosper."

We might ask, 'if God was with him, why didn't He deliver him?' God did eventually deliver him, but not until he had gone through the experiences God allowed in his life to prepare him to rule. Joseph didn't understand that at the time, but he continued to trust God on a daily basis and do his best with whatever his hand found to do.

New recruits in the armed forces are put through grueling training. It tests their endurance and their mental capacity. It is to prepare them for what comes in the heat of battle. It would be cruel and unfair to throw them into the battle with no preparation. So, God was preparing Joseph.

After awhile, the king's butler and baker were brought into prison and put under Joseph's charge. Each one had a dream that troubled him, and Joseph interpreted their dreams. He said in three days the chief butler would be returned to his duties, but the baker would be hanged. Both dreams came to pass just as Joseph had said. He asked the butler to please remember him and his cause to Pharaoh when he was restored to his position. But the butler forgot Joseph until two years later when Pharaoh had a dream and needed an interpretation. Then the butler remembered and told Pharaoh about Joseph and how he had interpreted their dreams precisely as they came about. Pharaoh called for Joseph to be brought to him immediately.

Of course, God gave Joseph the interpretation of Pharaoh's dreams. There would be seven years of plenty followed by seven years of famine. God also gave Joseph the wisdom to prepare for the famine. So, just like that, Joseph became second in command of Egypt, the most powerful nation in the then-known world. From a prisoner to a prince in a moment's time. Only Pharaoh had more power than Joseph.

They gathered grain during the years of plenty so there would be enough for everyone in the years of famine. When the famine came, Joseph was in charge of dispersing the grain. But this famine was not only in Egypt. It was all over the world. So, Joseph found himself saving the lives of the world…and His people, the Hebrews.

Sometimes God puts us in a place of service, but it's only for a season. Potiphar's house was not Joseph's destination. It was just one segment of his journey, just like living in Canaan with his family was one segment. God was positioning and training Joseph for the next level of service. He was advancing Joseph for His own purposes, although it looked strangely like defeat from Joseph's point of view. But if Potiphar and the jailer noticed God's hand of favor on Joseph, surely Joseph sensed His presence, too. He probably remembered the dreams and thought of them often. After all, God is the One Who gave him the dreams at the beginning.

Knowing God is with us helps us stay the course even when it looks like we are lost in a wilderness. The presence of God is our joy and comfort in the hard, perplexing times that come to us all. He is with us through the trials and tests that serve as our training ground. He never leaves us alone. So, regardless of the position we find ourselves in, we are to serve God with steadfastness and excellence.

Joseph had experienced brothers who hated him and sold him into slavery, a seductress who falsely accused him and landed him in prison, and then a butler who forgot him for two full years. None of these had mild consequences on Joseph's life. They were major shifts that brought harsh, unjust living conditions. He had a lot of chances to hold a grudge and a lot of time to plot revenge. Or he had a lot of chances to learn to forgive and trust God with the outcome.

Meanwhile, for the brothers back home, life had returned to its normal cadence. Surely there must have been times they felt a twinge of guilt about their evil deed against Joseph and about lying to their father, but that was in the past. What's done is done and life goes on. Until a famine came to their land. They probably thought Joseph was dead by now. But, whatever they thought, they had no idea he was in Egypt. Or that he was second in command there. Or that when they went to buy grain, they would meet him face to face. And he had power to do whatever he wanted to do to them with no questions asked. Life has a way of turning things around, especially when God is directing our steps. Joseph was about to get another test, too.

Jacob got word that there was grain in Egypt. Since the famine was in their land, too, he sent ten of his sons to Egypt to buy food. The same ten who sold Joseph all those years ago. Jacob would not allow Benjamin to go along because he was afraid of losing him like he had lost Joseph. He was still grieving for his son after all those years.

When the brothers arrived in Egypt, they bowed before Joseph and asked to buy grain. Joseph asked where they were from and about their family. He labeled them as spies. Joseph knew who they were, but they didn't recognize him. He probably looked very much Egyptian. He spoke roughly to them and told them to bring their youngest brother back with them to prove they were not spies. He held Simeon in prison in Egypt pending their return. The brothers spoke among themselves about all their troubles being caused by their actions against their brother Joseph so many years ago. They had no idea Joseph could understand them, because he had spoken to them through an interpreter. And now they had to go home and try to convince their father to let Benjamin to back with them. As if that wasn't bad enough, they found their money in the top of their food sacks on the way home. Now they could be accused of stealing!

Of course, when they returned home and told Jacob what had happened, he refused to allow Benjamin to go with them, even though Simeon had been left behind. It was not until their food was gone and they needed more to survive, that he relented. All this time Simeon was in an Egyptian prison. When the brothers finally returned to Egypt with Benjamin, Joseph had them eat a meal with him at his house, then he revealed his identity to them.

What a shock!! Can you imagine how they felt, knowing the power their brother wielded and the unfeeling act of injustice they had done against him? Terror may be too mild a word. They had no idea as they bowed to him when they came to get grain that first time as well as on this day that Joseph's dreams had become a reality.

What would happen to them now? They already suspected God was punishing them for their evil deeds, but this? They were trapped. Now they were at his mercy and they knew what they deserved. But they were in for another shock.

Look at Joseph's response to his brothers. "But now, do not be grieved or angry with yourselves because you sold me here; for God sent me before you to preserve life. For these two years the famine has been in the land, and there are still five years in which there will be neither plowing nor harvesting. And God sent me before you to preserve a posterity for you in the earth, and to save your lives by a great deliverance. So now it was not you who sent me here, but God; and He has made me a father to Pharaoh, and lord of all his house, and a ruler throughout all the land of Egypt." (Genesis 45:5-8) They had a family reunion instead of ten hangings. This family was put back together because of the hand of God on Joseph. I'm sure that had a much greater respect for him now.

Joseph recognized the hand of God in every event. Being sold into bondage in Egypt, getting experience when he was over Potiphar's household, serving in the prison and being connected to the chief butler. All of that was in God's plan. He was training Joseph to be forgiving and to accept life's seasons in faith at the hand of the Lord God Jehovah.

You can read the long version of this story in Genesis 37 and 39-50. As it turned out, Joseph moved his whole family from Canaan to Goshen in Egypt so he could take care of them during the remaining years of the famine. Jacob was elated to see Joseph again, and I imagine his brothers had some explaining to do. Everything seemed fine until Jacob died. Then the brothers, obviously still guilt-ridden, became apprehensive that Joseph hated them for what they had done to him and would get his revenge now that their father was dead.

"So they sent messengers to Joseph, saying, "Before your father died he commanded, saying, 'Thus you shall say to Joseph: "I beg you, please forgive the trespass of your brothers and their sin; for they did evil to you."' Now, please, forgive the trespass of the servants of the God of your father.

It sounds more like those were the words of Joseph's brothers, not their father's words. But regardless of the origin of the request, the brothers were obviously afraid for their lives.

Here, again, Joseph's response to his brothers is unexpected. "And Joseph wept when they spoke to him." When Joseph began to weep, "Then his brothers also went and fell down before his face, and they said, "Behold, we are your servants." Joseph had enough servants. He wanted brothers.

Joseph said to them, "Do not be afraid, for am I in the place of God? But as for you, you meant evil against me; but God meant it for good, in order to bring it about as it is this day, to save many people alive. Now therefore, do not be afraid; I will provide for you and your little ones." And he comforted them and spoke kindly to them. (Genesis 50:16-21)

After those years of all the family living in Egypt, they still had not learned to accept Joseph's forgiveness. They thought he had an ulterior motive to get even once their father was gone. They expected the "do not be grieved or angry with yourselves" speech to wear off and for revenge to come. It must have seemed unthinkable for someone as powerful as Joseph to truly forgive their terrible injustice to him. But Joseph had forgiven them, however they had not taken his advice. They neither accepted his forgiveness nor forgave themselves.

We don't know if Joseph's brothers were ever able to forgive themselves or not, but we do know Joseph understood enough about God to forgive them and to see God's mighty power cause their evil deed to work for good – their good and the good of the whole world.

Jesus said, "And whoever of you desires to be first shall be slave of all." (Mark 10:44) Greatness comes from having a servant's heart. Joseph learned that lesson well.

WHAT ABOUT ME?

Do we seek revenge when someone treats us unjustly or even cruelly? Or are we ready to forgive and recognize the hand of God in our lives? Some wounds may require a little "time off" for healing, but we should never allow wounds to fester and cause us to die spiritually or stop us from following Christ. He calls us to follow Him in the healing and forgiving ministry, and He will be with us through all the steps of preparation.

When we really believe that God is faithful to take the good and the bad and make something good out of it all, we can afford to let others off the hook, even if they don't deserve it. That is what Christ has done for us. We can never repay Him. But we can follow His lead and be people of mercy and compassion, giving the same grace that has been extended to us.

> *"Therefore, If your enemy is hungry, feed him; If he is thirsty, give him a drink; For in so doing you will heap coals of fire on his head." Do not be overcome by evil, but overcome evil with good."*
> Romans 12:20-21

How eager am I to heal the wounds of those who have hurt me?

When I am mistreated and neglected, do I refuse to bring healing to others, or do I reach out in love?

Do I try to make sure they suffer at least a little bit, or do I leave it in God's hands?

Is there someone in my life that I need to forgive?

WORD STUDY

Enemy – one who is actively against another

Coals of fire – symbolic of bringing about conviction that leads to repentance

Overcome – conquer; defeat

Evil – morally wrong; wicked

Chapter Nine

HOPELESSNESS – HAGAR

> **HOPELESSNESS**
>
> **without hope; desperate; to feel one is doomed; destined for an adverse fate**

While I was at a college for a writers' workshop, I went down to the next floor of the building to avoid the line at the ladies' room. I was alone as I walked down the stairs, through the hallway, into one room and then another. I was the only one on that floor. Suddenly, the lights went out, and it was pitch dark. It was so dark I couldn't see how to get out. I felt my way through one room and finally found the door. The next room was just as dark…until I saw a tiny, pinpoint light blinking. It was on the far wall, and I knew it was the light switch by the door. I started making my way toward it, and when it sensed my presence, light flooded the room. I could clearly see my surroundings once again. And I walked confidently back to the conference room for the next session.

Are you walking in darkness today, trying to find the way out? If you will look, there is a tiny light blinking. It is called Hope. When you start toward it, Jesus will flood your life with His light. All you have to do is turn to Him and He will show you the way. Jesus is our Hope, and He is the light shining on our path so we can walk with confidence in Him.

Hagar's story is a sad one that she thought was hopeless and was about to end tragically. She probably felt like she was groping in darkness, but Hope shone His light on her. God heard her cry in the wilderness on two occasions. He made a promise to Hagar concerning her son for the future, and provided the water and direction for them in the present. Her story clearly reveals that God sees, God hears, and God speaks. When God speaks, miracles happen and creative forces go to work. We are not without hope.

****

Hagar was an Egyptian slave girl belonging to a woman of great wealth. Hagar's name means "flight" or "turning". And that meaning would prove to be the pattern of her life. The name of Hagar's mistress was Sarah and her husband's name was Abraham. God had made a covenant with Abraham and promised him a son through Sarah. He also promised him descendants that would be more than the sand on the seashore or the stars in the sky. But the couple was advanced in age and still had no son. Hagar probably had heard of how God had spoken to Abraham, although she had no idea just how caught up in this promise she would become. But she was soon to find out.

After years went by with no son, Sarah told Abraham that since God had kept her from having a child, maybe she could have a child through Hagar. The child of such a union would belong to the owner of the slave-girl in those days. That would be Sarah. So, Sarah gave Hagar to Abraham as a secondary wife, a type of surrogate mother for Sarah's child. That would provide Abraham with the son God had promised, so they thought. Abraham agreed to the plan, and when Hagar knew she was with child, she regarded her mistress with contempt and disrespect.

Sarah blamed Abraham for Hagar's arrogant behavior. But Abraham simply told Sarah that Hagar was her maid and she could do whatever she pleased with her. Sarah treated Hagar harshly, so Hagar ran away from Sarah.

Hagar must have felt very alone. She had not volunteered to be part of this plan of Sarah's. She wasn't even considered and had no choice in the matter. Her life had been completely up-ended and she must have felt terribly helpless, hopeless and mistreated. There is no mention of Abraham or any of his servants going out looking for her. It seems no one sought her out to make sure she was alright. Except One. The Angel of the Lord found her by a fountain of water in the wilderness on the road that led to Egypt, her home country. Many theologians believe this Angel was the pre-incarnate Christ, the Son of God Himself. When He asked Hagar where she had come from and where she was going, she told Him she was running away from Sarah, her mistress. Her answer was honest and direct.

The Angel of the Lord told her to go back to Sarah and to submit to her. What a difficult thing to do. Yet, Hagar's choices were almost non-existent. She was more vulnerable now that she was expecting a baby than she ever had been and probably wouldn't make it all the way to Egypt anyway. She was caught in the middle of a plan that should never have been implemented. And it seemed that, so far, she was not handling it well.

Sometimes, even when we had nothing to do with creating a bad situation, we can make it worse with a wrong attitude, disrespectful words and rebellious actions. It takes a strong person to admit their wrong and make it right, especially when they, too, have been wronged. Hagar needed direction and hope. She received both. After telling her to go back and submit, "the Angel of the Lord said to her, 'I will greatly multiply your descendants so that they will be too many to count'" And the Angel of the Lord continued, "Behold, you are with child, and you will bear a son; and you shall name him Ishmael (God hears), Because the Lord has heard and paid attention to your persecution (suffering)." God is never blind to our problems. He is not deaf to our cries. He sees when we are hurt and confused. He knows when we are on the run to return to our old life and territory. And He loves us too much to let us go. When it seems darkness has overtaken us, Jesus sheds light on our path to bring us out.

Hagar called the Lord who spoke to her the "God Who Sees;" for she said, "Have I not even here [in the wilderness] remained alive after seeing Him [who sees me with understanding and compassion]?" (Amplified Bible) The name in Hebrew is El-roi – "God never sleeps, He sees, He is aware, He is the great Omnipresent God."

In our greatest victories, our worst defeats, our greatest joys and deepest sorrows, He is there. We need to open our eyes to see Him and unstop our ears to hear Him. We are not without hope or resources unless we refuse His extended hand. Even today, Jesus invites us to Himself. We can stop going through all the religious rituals that leave us more hopeless than we were before. We can come into His presence and be refreshed and renewed by Him. We can learn from Him as we live in His presence, following His instructions with a humble heart. When we live daily in His presence, we will find rest and peace for our souls. Our hope will be renewed.

Hagar found that peace and guidance in God's presence, and she followed the instructions of the Angel of the Lord. She returned to Sarah and later gave birth to Abraham's son. The Scripture tells us that Abraham named his son Ishmael. Perhaps Hagar told him about her meeting with the Angel of the Lord. Or possibly God Himself told Abraham. We don't know, but we do know his name was Ishmael, just as the Angel of the Lord told Hagar. Abraham was eighty-six years old when Ishmael was born.

Abraham and Sarah had stepped out of God's will to produce the promised son. But Ishmael was not Sarah's son, and he was not the son God had promised. God spoke to Abraham again and told him Sarah would have a son named Isaac. Abraham was 100 years old and Sarah was 90 when Isaac was born. Sarah and Abraham were full of joy.

But before long, there was more trouble for Hagar and Ishmael. When Isaac was weaned, they had a big party for him. Sarah saw Ishmael mocking Isaac and she told Abraham, "Drive out this maid and her son, for the son of this maid shall not be an heir with my son Isaac."

Abraham was terribly upset and displeased with Sarah's demand because Ishmael was his son, even if he was not the son of promise. But God told him to send them away and that He would make a nation from Ishmael because he was Abraham's descendant. However, God's promise was through Isaac as He had spoken from the beginning.

So, Abraham gave Hagar food and water and sent them away. Ishmael would have been about fourteen years old when Isaac was born, so he may have been sixteen or seventeen when he was sent away.

How many more sharp turns could Hagar's life take? Here she was, having to 'take flight' again. Here she was alone and hopeless all over again. She had been rejected and now she was wandering in the wilderness. When the food and water were gone, she put Ishmael under a shrub and she went and sat down across from him a short distance away so she wouldn't have to watch him die. As she sat there, she began to cry. "And God heard the voice of the lad." An angel of God called out to Hagar from heaven and asked her what was wrong. Without waiting for an answer, he said, "Fear not, for God has heard the voice of the lad where he is. Arise, lift up the lad and hold him with your hand, for I will make him a great nation." I can almost see Hagar getting up and helping Ishmael to stand, all the while supporting him with her hand. It was probably hot there in the desert sun, but Hagar had heard from God. That made all the difference.

I wonder what Ishmael had been saying when God heard his voice. That is something we just don't know. But we do know God heard him and sent help. Then God opened Hagar's eyes, and she saw a well of water. She gave Ishmael a drink and he revived.

Sometimes the provision we need is right before us, but we are too discouraged and weary to see it until God opens our eyes. There are times we need to be reminded of what God has promised us, especially when we hit another bump in the road and it seems there is no way His promise can come to pass. Life can seem pretty bleak, dark and hopeless sometimes, but we cannot expect to ever find any real hope in this world. We have to look up for that. Then we can be refreshed by the water of God's Spirit. Our only hope is in Jesus. If you need a reminder of what He promised, just read His Word, listen to biblical messages, and listen to the voice of the Holy Spirit as He brings to our remembrance what Jesus has said.

God often meets us right where we are. Especially when He knows we have gone as far as our own strength can take us. Isaiah 40:28-31 gives us this encouragement. "Have you not known? Have you not heard? The everlasting God, the Lord, The Creator of the ends of the earth, neither faints nor is weary. His understanding is unsearchable. He gives power to the weak, and to those who have no might He increases strength. Even the youths shall faint and be weary, And the young men shall utterly fall, but those who wait on the Lord Shall renew their strength; They shall mount up with wings like eagles, they shall run and not be weary, they shall walk and not faint." When we are weak, He is strong. We can draw from that strength and keep going.

As the years went by, Ishmael grew and became an archer. His mother took a wife for him from Egypt, and that is the last we hear from Hagar. But God was with Ishmael just as He said He would be, and He made a great nation from him. Ishmael lived in the wilderness of Paran, and his lineage is listed in Genesis 25:12-18. His descendants, the Arab nations, are still among us today. And just as Isaac, the son of promise had twelve sons, Ishmael also had twelve sons, or princes as the King James Version calls them.

When Abraham was 175 years old, he "breathed his last and died in a good old age, an old man and full of years, and was gathered to his people. And his sons Isaac and Ishmael buried him in the cave of Machpelah, which is before Mamre, in the field of Ephron the son of Zohar the Hittite," (Genesis 25:8-9)

Matthew Henry wrote, "His sons buried him. It was the last office of respect they had to pay to their good father. Some distance there had formerly been between Isaac and Ishmael; but it seems either that Abraham had brought them together while he lived, or at least that his death reconciled them. Although Abraham had other children by his wife Keturah (which he married after the death of Sarah), Isaac and Ishmael are the only sons who are mentioned who came to bury their father.

Ishmael was 137 years old when he died.

****

WHAT ABOUT ME?

If we draw near to Jesus, He will draw near to us. He shows us enough of the right way to let us make our decision to follow, or continue to wander in the wilderness. When we make a step in His direction, He will give us all the light we need. All obscurity is removed and we can see Him clearly. And we can be sure that whatever He promises will come to pass.

> *"This hope" [our hope in Christ] "we have as an anchor of the soul, both sure and steadfast, and which enters the Presence behind the veil."* Hebrews 6:19

Where do I put my trust when it seems I am wandering aimlessly without any direction or hope?

Am I trusting in my own thoughts and emotions, or am I looking for the spark of light that Jesus offers?

Have I determined to follow Jesus once I see His light?

WORD STUDY

Anchor – a device that causes something to be fixed in place, securing it

Soul – mind, will, and emotions

Sure – confident assurance, free from doubt, fully persuaded

Steadfast – firmly fixed, unwavering

Veil – the separation agent between us and God

Chapter Ten

PAGAN CULTURE - DANIEL

> **PAGAN**
> serving false gods rather than the one true God; replacing worship of Jehovah with idol worship

One day I was preparing potatoes to bake. My husband was grilling steaks and it was the perfect side dish. I went through my normal routine, scrubbing the outside of the potatoes, pricking each of them with a fork, then rubbing them in olive oil. Just before I put them into the oven to bake, I covered them with foil.

As I was going through the process, I thought of our lives. When we are saved, we are washed by God's Spirit. Then come the testing times of our lives that seem to prick us on every hand. But the oil of the Holy Spirit is applied to us and we sense His presence. He covers us even in the heat of persecution and presents us as useful vessels to sustain others in their walk with Him, just as He has sustained us.

At a young age, Daniel was taken captive to Babylon. He was subjected to the training and ways of the Babylonians and was surrounded with ungodliness in a pagan nation. However, Daniel did not allow his environment to change his commitment to the Lord God Jehovah. He continued to pray and seek God, regardless of the risk that was sometimes involved. As a result, he was given many opportunities to be used as a vessel showing God's glory to kings and servants in his pagan surroundings.

Daniel shows us that the test of our integrity lies not only in the difficult struggles in our lives, but also the times we are bestowed with prestige, honor and favor. That could certainly turn the head of a young man like Daniel, but it didn't. He was steadfast in His devotion to God whether taking a stand that would risk his life or enjoying peace and honor.

****

Probably one of the most heartbreaking days etched in Daniel's mind was the day his city, Jerusalem, was attacked by enemies, destroyed and burned. What a tragic experience for a young man to live through. But to add to the horror of the attack, now the enemy army was leading Daniel away from everything familiar to him. Suddenly he was among the captives being taken to a foreign land as slaves. Many were left behind in the rubble of what used to be their city. But not Daniel.

Daniel was in a category of young men that Nebuchadnezzar had ordered his chief official, Ashpenaz, to bring back to Babylon with him. Here is the description of the ones he wanted: "some from the royal family and from the nobles, young men without blemish and handsome in appearance, skillful in all wisdom, endowed with intelligence and discernment, and quick to understand, competent to stand [in the presence of the king] and able to serve in the king's palace." (Daniel 1:3-4 Amplified)

So, Daniel was uprooted from his native land, his family and the temple of His God, Jehovah. He probably had dreams of growing up in his spiritual culture and worshiping God among his people, but God had something greater.

There was another power who had plans for Daniel, too. King Nebuchadnezzar. He ordered Ashpenaz to teach these young captives "the literature and language of the Chaldeans. The king assigned a daily ration for them from his finest food and from the wine which he drank. They were to be educated and nourished this way for three years so that at the end of that time, they were prepared to enter the king's service. Among them from the sons of Judah were: Daniel, Hananiah, Mishael and Azariah."

One of the first things to change, besides their residence, were their names. Each of these young men was given a Babylonian name. Daniel was now Belteshazzar. Hananiah was Shadrach, Mishael was named Meshach and Azariah was now Abednego. It seemed they were well on their way to being acclimated to the Babylonian way of life. They were considered young and easy to bend. But changing their names did not change who they really were, and these four young men were worshipers of Jehovah and followed His laws.

One of the first problems they encountered was being served the king's food. What the king ate had first been offered to idols and was also food they as Jews were forbidden by God to eat. They purposed in their hearts not to defile themselves with the king's food. But how could they get around it? God gave Daniel favor with Ashpenaz, so Daniel asked him to please let them eat something else so they would not defile themselves. At first the official was hesitant because he did not want to go against the king's commandment and lose his life. But when Daniel suggested a trial period, he agreed. At the end of that trial, when the four young men looked healthier than the others who were eating the king's food, Ashpenaz changed their diets.

God's plan for Daniel was greater than the plan of Nebuchadnezzar. When we are in the will of God and have purposed in our hearts to follow Him regardless of our culture, He will open doors that we cannot open for ourselves. He is faithful.

The day finally arrived for these young men to be presented to the king. "The king spoke with them, and among them all not one was found like Daniel, Hananiah, Mishael, and Azariah; so they were [selected and] assigned to stand before the king and enter his personal service. In every matter of wisdom and understanding about which the king consulted them, he found them ten times better than all the [learned] magicians and enchanters (Magi) in his whole realm." (Daniel 1:19-20 Amplified Bible)

Daniel would remain in Babylon the rest of his life and serving under four different kings over the course of seventy years. He served in the palace under Nebuchadnezzar, Belshazzar, Darius and Cyrus. His service to them was with honor and integrity, but his first allegiance remained with the Lord God Jehovah.

How could Daniel stand in such a hostile environment? How could he serve pagan kings and yet remain unscathed by their idols and the culture that was ingrained in them? Because the love of God and service to Him was ingrained in Daniel's heart. He had purposed to do what was right in God's eyes even if it meant death from the reigning earthly king. When the circumstance arrived that called for a decision, Daniel's decision had already been made. God came first. Yet he gave these kings the honor they deserved in their positions.

One night Nebuchadnezzar dreamed a dream that disturbed him and he asked all the wise men to tell him what the dream was and the interpretation. None could do it. They declared to the king that no king had ever demanded such a thing from his wise men. Nebuchadnezzar was so enraged that he ordered all his wise men to be killed. Daniel heard about the problem and asked for a little time to seek God about this mystery.

Daniel went to his house and told Hananiah, Mishael, and Azariah about the king's order that would directly affect them as they would be killed along with the other wise men. He asked them to pray with him that God would reveal the secret to him. When God revealed the mystery to Daniel in a night vision, the first thing Daniel did was to worship God, even before he went to tell Nebuchadnezzar and save their lives. He said, "Blessed be the name of God forever and ever, for wisdom and might are His. And He changes the times and the seasons; He removes kings and raises up kings; He gives wisdom to the wise and knowledge to those who have understanding. He reveals deep and secret things; He knows what is in the darkness, and light dwells with Him. I thank You and praise You, O God of my fathers; You have given me wisdom and might, and have now made known to me what we asked of You, for You have made known to us the king's demand." (Daniel 2:20-23)

God was faithful to show Daniel the dream. That is why Daniel was faithful to praise God for His mercy and wisdom.

God used Daniel to save the lives of all the wise men in Babylon. What if Daniel had not stayed in touch with God? What if he had succumbed to the culture around him? He would have been as weak and unknowledgeable as all the others. But he chose not to compromise his relationship with God. We can do that, too. It may be difficult, but if we choose to be faithful to God in all things, great and small, He will see us through.

Daniel was careful to give the honor where it belonged when he went before the king. He gave the honor to God and God alone. Daniel went before Nebuchadnezzar and said, "The secret which the king has demanded, the wise men, the astrologers, the magicians, and the soothsayers cannot declare to the king. But there is a God in heaven who reveals secrets, and He has made known to King Nebuchadnezzar what will be in the latter days. Your dream, and the visions of your head upon your bed, were these: As for you, O king, thoughts came to your mind while on your bed, about what would come to pass after this; and He who reveals secrets has made known to you what will be. But as for me, this secret has not been revealed to me because I have more wisdom than anyone living, but for our sakes who make known the interpretation to the king, and that you may know the thoughts of your heart." (Daniel 2:27-30)

Daniel had no grand illusions of himself as some great man who had acquired personal supernatural powers to do these things. He knew it was God working through him to get this message to Nebuchadnezzar. We do well when we remember we are but dust, and anything God does through us is for His honor and glory, and not our own. We have great power within us if we are indwelt by the Holy Spirit. But we are only earthen vessels. He is the treasure within us.

When king Nebuchadnezzar heard Daniel describe his dream and then explain the interpretation, he began to give praise to Daniel's God. He fell prostrate on the floor and said, "Surely your God is the God of gods and the Lord of kings and a revealer of mysteries, for you were able to reveal this mystery." Then he made Daniel ruler over the entire province of Babylon and put him in charge of all his wise men. He also gave extravagant gifts to Daniel. Then through Daniel's recommendation, Shadrach, Meshach and Abednego were made administrators.

Can we stay faithful to God through it all? The good, the bad, and the everyday? Can we accept honor and power and still humble ourselves before God? Daniel was a man of integrity. He stood firmly on the principles of God. His character was sound in morals and unmoving in his faith in God. He was honest and consistent in his commitment to God. He was authentic. And he had purposed in his heart not to defile himself in any way.

That first dream was one that honored Nebuchadnezzar. He was the head of gold, and the kingdoms coming after him would diminish in power and glory. That was probably the idea for the statue Nebuchadnezzar made, requiring everyone to bow to it. So much for giving God the glory. But that day would come.

Nebuchadnezzar had several glimpses of God's glory through these young men from the tribe of Judah. He saw the unmatched power of their God when he watched as God saved Shadrach, Meshach and Abednego from the fiery furnace. He actually saw the Lord in the furnace with them. When they came out, he saw that they were not burned, their clothes were not burned and they didn't even smell of smoke. But God would deal with Nebuchadnezzar yet again, and He chose to warn him in a dream that Daniel would be called on to interpret.

This next dream was concerning an event to come, but it was a warning of personal judgment on king Nebuchadnezzar. It was very unlike the first dream. This dream caused Nebuchadnezzar to be afraid. He would be brought low, very low. The king would be driven from his kingdom. He would have the mind and nature of a wild animal and eat grass. He would live with the beasts in the field for seven years. Then he would be reinstated to his kingdom.

How could Daniel possibly tell the king all this? This was terrible news. But he faithfully and honestly delivered the message from God. Daniel said he wished the dream was meant for Nebuchadnezzar's enemies, but it was definitely meant for him. After interpreting the dream, Daniel offered this advice. "Therefore, O king, let my advice to you be [considered and found] acceptable; break away now from your sins and exhibit your repentance by doing what is right, and from your wickedness by showing mercy to the poor, so that [if you repent] there may possibly be a continuance of your prosperity and tranquility and a healing of your error.'" (Daniel 4:27 Amplified Bible)

Daniel was brave to speak God's words to the king, knowing it would distress him and possibly anger him. An angry king often kills the messenger. Yet Daniel spoke the words God gave him of the impending judgment. But Daniel went further than that. He was compassionate and bold to offer Nebuchadnezzar a possible escape. Even though he was offering good advice, it was dangerous to speak of the king's sin, error and wickedness. But Nebuchadnezzar did not take Daniel's advice.

Are we willing to speak to others when it might make them angry or cause us to appear to think we are better than they are? Are we loving enough to speak the truth even at the risk of being misunderstood to give them the chance to turn things around? Many are offended by the truth, but many are set free by that same truth when it is spoken with love. We are to be truth bearers.

One day, as Nebuchadnezzar was looking out over the kingdom of Babylon, he began bragging about his kingdom and his power that had brought it all into being. Immediately his dream came to pass. It is amazing to me that he would be allowed to return to his throne after such a mental breakdown that lasted seven years. But God is God and He determines it all. Truly, God puts kings on their thrones and removes them at His will.

When Nebuchadnezzar returned to his kingdom, he had this to say: "And at the end of the time I, Nebuchadnezzar, lifted my eyes to heaven, and my understanding returned to me; and I blessed the Most High and praised and honored Him who lives forever: For His dominion is an everlasting dominion, And His kingdom is from generation to generation. All the inhabitants of the earth are reputed as nothing; He does according to His will in the army of heaven and among the inhabitants of the earth. No one can restrain His hand or say to Him, "What have You done?" At the same time my reason returned to me, and for the glory of my kingdom, my honor and splendor returned to me. My counselors and nobles resorted to me, I was restored to my kingdom, and excellent majesty was added to me. Now I, Nebuchadnezzar, praise and extol and honor the King of heaven, all of whose works are truth, and His ways justice. And those who walk in pride He is able to put down." (Daniel 4:34-37)

Finally, Nebuchadnezzar bowed before God. He did not just give Him an "honorable mention". He knew God's power and His glory firsthand from seven years of experience.

Daniel would go on to serve king Belshazzar (Nebuchadnezzar's grandson) only on the occasion of his demise and the takeover of Jerusalem by King Darius. It appears that Belshazzar had not called on Daniel's wisdom or his God before that night. But when a hand began writing on the wall, interrupting his feast, Belshazzar was baffled and afraid. The Queen mother suggested he call in Daniel. So, Daniel was called to interpret the handwriting on the wall. But before he interpreted it, he recounted the story of what had happened to Nebuchadnezzar when he disregarded God. Then he continued like this.

"But you his son, Belshazzar, have not humbled your heart, although you knew all this. And you have lifted yourself up against the Lord of heaven. They have brought the vessels of His house before you, and you and your lords, your wives and your concubines, have drunk wine from them. And you have praised the gods of silver and gold, bronze and iron, wood and stone, which do not see or hear or know; and the God who holds your breath in His hand and owns all your ways, you have not glorified. Then the fingers of the hand were sent from Him, and this writing was written. "And this is the inscription that was written: MENE, MENE, TEKEL, UPHARSIN. This is the interpretation of each word.

MENE: God has numbered your kingdom, and finished it;
TEKEL: You have been weighed in the balances, and found wanting;
PERES: Your kingdom has been divided, and given to the Medes and Persians."

"Then Belshazzar gave the command, and they clothed Daniel with purple and put a chain of gold around his neck, and made a proclamation concerning him that he should be the third ruler in the kingdom. That very night Belshazzar, king of the Chaldeans, was slain. And Darius the Mede received the kingdom, being about sixty-two years old." (Daniel 5:22-30)

Belshazzar's warning was his grandfather's experience. He ignored it and paid a tremendous price. He lost the kingdom and his life. He might have lived in peace if he had learned the lesson of God's power from Nebuchadnezzar. But he didn't.

Daniel was kept in the new king's service. God was not finished with Daniel by far. He served Darius well and Darius was about to promote him, but some of the other leaders who were jealous of Daniel told the king that all of the rulers in his kingdom had consulted together to make a firm decree that no one could make any petition of any God or man for thirty days, excepting the king. Anyone who did so would be thrown into the den of lions. But one of the chief rulers was not consulted about that decree. They had purposely left out Daniel.

These men could find no other way to get rid of Daniel. There was nothing out of order with his work, his service or his integrity. But they knew he prayed to Jehovah three times a day. So, they came up with a law against his prayers, knowing Daniel would continue to pray to his God. Once the law had been sealed by the king, it could not be reversed. Daniel would go into the lion's den and they would be rid of him. At least that was their plan. They were not counting on the Lord intervening on Daniel's behalf.

After Daniel heard about the king's command, he had a choice to make. He could obey the king or obey God. But that choice had been made many years before. Daniel continued to open his window toward Jerusalem and pray to the Lord Jehovah three times a day. His accusers were there to witness his prayers and to arrest him.

Although the king tried to find a way to keep Daniel from the lion's den, they found no legal way to change the law. Darius had no idea when they came to him with their "decree" that it was a scheme to kill Daniel. He didn't realize until it was too late that they had tricked him.

After a night in the lion's den for Daniel and a sleepless night for the king, Darius went early the next morning to the lion's den and cried out to Daniel. He said, "Daniel, servant of the living God, has your God, whom you serve continually, been able to deliver you from the lions?" What a relief it must have been for Darius to hear Daniel's voice answering him from the lion's den. Daniel said, "O king, live forever! My God sent His angel and shut the lions' mouths, so that they have not hurt me, because I was found innocent before Him; and also, O king, I have done no wrong before you. Now the king was exceedingly glad for him, and commanded that they should take Daniel up out of the den. So, Daniel was taken up out of the den, and no injury whatever was found on him, because he believed in his God." (Daniel 6:21-23)

Daniel came out of the lion's den unscathed. His accusers did not have the same results when they were thrown in among the lions. God protected Daniel and was glorified. The king was a very happy man because Daniel was safe and the truth had won out over evil. Obviously, Darius cared for Daniel and believed that His God could save him. Daniel was a vessel used by God to show the glory of God to these kings and to all the others he influenced during his service in the palace at Babylon.

Daniel's service to king Cyrus was his last in Babylon. But with all four of the kings, from the time he was a young man until his old age, God was with him. He gave Daniel favor because He knew He could trust Daniel to stay true to God above all else, even risking his own life.

King Cyrus allowed the Jewish captives to go back to Jerusalem and rebuild it. By that time Daniel would have probably been too old to make the long journey, but he had done his part in God's plan right there in Babylon. It was Daniel who studied out the prophecy of Jeremiah telling the time of the captives' release. When he realized it was time according to the prophecy, he began to pray a prayer of repentance and a plea to God to release His people to go back to Jerusalem to rebuild. Daniel knew it was prophesied, so he agreed with God and set in motion the return of the Jews to their homeland.

1 John 5:14-15 tells us, "Now this is the confidence that we have in Him, that if we ask anything according to His will, He hears us. And if we know that He hears us, whatever we ask, we know that we have the petitions that we have asked of Him." When we are close to God and study the Scripture, we can know how to pray and release the captives.

Daniel was consistently true to God even while in service to pagan kings for seventy years. We can follow his example by not compromising God's principles. Because Daniel gave himself completely to God, he was used greatly by God. God can do the same with anyone who is surrendered to Him.

Even while serving the kings of Babylon, God entrusted Daniel with many visions concerning future events. Daniel was visited by the angel Gabriel who showed him many things that are included in the book of Daniel. Some of those prophecies have been fulfilled and some are yet to come. Daniel's influence remains among us through his example and his writings.

I am reminded of a song we used to sing frequently. One verse says, "I have decided to follow Jesus. No turning back. No turning back." Let that be our resolve.

****

WHAT ABOUT ME?

We can shine the light of Jesus Christ even in a pagan society. We can make a difference when we don't compromise God's principles. We don't have to make a big show of it, just simply follow God's Word and the Holy Spirit's leading. We can be like Daniel who purposed in his heart not to defile himself with the things of the world around him, but to allow God to freely work through him.

"But we have this treasure in earthen vessels, that the excellence of the power may be of God and not of us." (2 Corinthians 4:7)

Have I purposed in my heart to follow Jesus, regardless of the cost?

Can I handle adversity and prosperity with integrity and steadfastness in my faith?

Is it an option in my mind to compromise if I am confronted with critical circumstances? Or has the decision already been settled to follow Jesus?

WORD STUDY

Treasure – spiritual riches, the infilling of the Holy Spirit

Earthen – of this world, composed of earth

Excellence – greatness, superiority

Power – capability, strength, authority, control

EPILOGUE

> **DISAPPOINT**
>
> fail to fulfill the wishes of; to have one's expectations unrealized

When I was diagnosed with cancer several years ago, my first words were "I don't have time for this!" I know that sounds like a senseless response, but my family and I were approaching a very busy time in our ministry and I was already in preparation mode. The kind, but firm, answer from the nurse was, "you are going to have to *make* time for it." She was right and I knew it. I just needed to come to terms with the facts, and that my plans would have to be altered. I didn't feel panicked or even surprised. At that moment, I was more concerned about the interruption in my life than I was about the possible outcome. I'm not sure exactly why.

I called my husband on my way home and asked him to meet us (my mother was with me) at a little restaurant in our city. A local pastor that I knew was there when we arrived, so while I waited for my husband, I told him about my diagnosis. He prayed with me right then and there. God's people are wonderful!

After consulting with an oncologist, the prognosis seemed pretty good. I would have surgery and thirty-six radiation treatments. I was very grateful that the surgery would not be as extensive as it could have been and that chemotherapy was not in the picture. I began praying and asking God to heal me as the surgery day approached. I read books on healing along with the Scripture. The biopsies had shown two spots that needed removing, and the surgeon felt confident it could be done completely.

There was one more procedure to be done the day of the surgery along with a scan just before I went over to the hospital. I was counting on that scan showing no cancer and the surgery being canceled. Instead of hearing "the cancer is gone", I overheard the doctor talking to someone else in the room about three spots. I couldn't believe my ears! I was praying for no cancer, not another area to be removed.

Have you ever been disappointed because God didn't do what you asked Him to do? Especially when you knew it would bring Him glory? It didn't make any sense to me. I left that clinic on my way to the hospital very upset, distressed and disappointed. So many people were praying for me and I knew God was in control. I just needed to get over the disappointment from not getting a 'yes' to my prayer. I wasn't afraid because I was too disappointed that this was not going the way I had it all planned. I had no idea what was still ahead for me.

After surgery, I returned to the same oncologist who was highly disturbed that cancer had been found in a lymph node (although it had been removed). He told me I needed a much more drastic surgery and chemotherapy. I was numb when I heard that. When I went back to the surgeon, I explained what the oncologist had said and how the treatment plans had changed since the surgery. I knew he was confident that he had removed all the cancer and the margins were good, although he didn't say it that day. He simply asked if I wanted a second opinion. Of course, I said 'yes' and was sent to another cancer specialist. After seeing a new doctor who had gone over all my records, I was given much better news. I needed no further surgery and no chemotherapy. I underwent all the radiation treatments and did very well with them. To God be the glory!

I would like to add that there were numerous people who were faithfully praying for me and with me during the whole ordeal, and I am so thankful for their persistence and encouragement. We need our brothers and sisters in Christ to help strengthen us when we are weak.

God does not always do things the way we ask Him to do them. He knows what we need and He allows only what He can use for our ultimate good. He doesn't always rescue us from the fire. Sometimes He just walks with us through it. We can trust Him even when we cannot understand. Nothing can thwart His plans or take Him by surprise. We can depend on His faithfulness in our lives. I praise Him for rescuing me from an unnecessary course of action! And I praise Him for teaching me more about His faithfulness in the storm. He doesn't give in to our wishes like a parent giving in to a spoiled child. He loves us too much to leave us to our own devices. He guides us in the way that is right for us. Not the easiest.

Charles Spurgeon wrote, "God is too good to be unkind and He is too wise to be mistaken. And when we cannot trace His hand, we must trust His heart."

There are many times in our lives we have to trust. There are many times we will go through disappointments and hardship and even persecution. But God is never far away. He is always right there with His children. We have His promise. "And the LORD, He *is* the One who goes before you. He will be with you, He will not leave you nor forsake you; do not fear nor be dismayed."

Trust in His love when the storms come and the battle gets hot. Trust in Jesus when the disappointments make you feel hopeless and when life seems unjust. Keep your trust in Him when everything is going great, because that is the time you are most vulnerable to begin to trust in yourself or other people. Trust Him when you feel like a failure or your plans have been interrupted. Trust Him when your circumstances seem to push you down or you find yourself in the middle of unbelievers who try to remake you into their image. Trust Him when you are rejected and when you are just plain tired. My friend, trust His heart and stand firmly in your place. You are a victor because Jesus Christ is victorious.

When is it time to quit, you may ask? Never, never, never, allow giving up to be an option! Stand when you feel you can stand no longer, because Jesus Christ will renew your strength and give you a second wind just when you think you are going to faint. It will be worth it all to see Jesus and hear Him say, "Well done my good and faithful servant."

D. L. Moody said, "it may be that some of us will be ushered very soon into the presence of the King. One gaze at Him will be enough to reward us for all we have had to bear. Yes, there is peace for the past, grace for the present, and glory for the future." Never forget that!

"Therefore do not cast away your confidence, which has great reward. For you have need of endurance, so that after you have done the will of God, you may receive the promise." (Hebrews 10:35-36)

The Mighty Conqueror

What is life and what its length?
Like treading water lest we sink?
Holding one's own and biding the time
Until death comes to stop the climb?

Or is there more beyond this life?
Beyond the labor and the strife?
Is there more beyond the grave,
Where the heart is not afraid?

There's a place of light and peace,
A place with God where troubles cease.
In God's sweet presence we can stay,
Safe in His kingdom every day.

Though this world shakes and turmoil swirls,
Though evil plots and plans are hurled,
Our hearts can rest in God alone
For He still sits upon His throne.

God is always in control.
In His mighty hand He holds
Every star and ocean wide,
This whole earth where we abide.

He sees the smallest bird that sings,
Yet His word rules the mighty kings.
He determines if they rise
Or if they come to their demise.

Falling mountains, raging seas,
All the Mighty God will please.
All of nature, every man
Will obey His just commands.

None can stop His wise decrees.
All will fall down on their knees
On that day when Christ shall reign.
Lord of lords and King of kings!

By Patti Hedgepath Lusk

Don't Miss These Titles from Patti Hedgepath Lusk

JUST A MINUTE

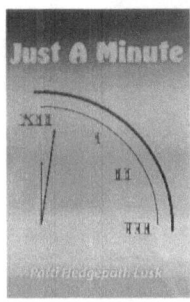

Are you lacking something in your spiritual life? We could all use some encouragement along the way, and it is usually right in front of us. Patti has taken ordinary happenings from real life occurrences and turned them into parables for today's living. What do beta fish, piano lessons, splinters and dessert have in common? They can all be learning experiences to lead us closer to Jesus.

ISBN 978-1-4276-2251-8

GOD'S ORDER

God's Order brings you back to God's foundational design for man and the world. These basic principles, once common knowledge in the church, have been reinterpreted by today's secular society. Discover the thread of order within the Scriptures as it weaves its way from Creation to God's plan for marriage, family, redemption, His church, and throughout eternity.

ISBN 978-1-61638-171-4

JUST A MINUTE: A Daily Challenge to Change

What can we learn from cardboard boxes, traffic lights, keys and alarm clocks? More than you might think! Parables and word pictures are enlightening means of transmitting God's Word from a page to our hearts. This book offers down-to-earth examples of spiritual truths that will open hearts to God and allow His Word to change us.

ISBN 978-0-692-95705-9

Available at www.amazon.com.

Email: counterfloministries@hotmail.com

www.counterfloministries.com

ABOUT THE AUTHOR

Patti Hedgepath Lusk is cofounder of CounterFlo Ministries. Along with her husband Scott and son Carlin, they share the gospel message through concerts, speaking engagements, books and other media. Patti is a frequent host on Nite Line, Dove Broadcasting's flagship program. She is also a columnist for her local paper, the Belton-Honea Path News Chronicle. For more information visit www.counterfloministries.com. Or pattihlusk.blogspot.com.

www.ingramcontent.com/pod-product-compliance
Lightning Source LLC
Chambersburg PA
CBHW021412290426
44108CB00010B/496